# AppleScript Scripting Additions Guide

**English Dialect**

**Addison-Wesley Publishing Company**

Reading, Massachusetts   Menlo Park, California   New York
Don Mills, Ontario   Wokingham, England   Amsterdam   Bonn
Sydney   Singapore   Tokyo   Madrid   San Juan
Paris   Seoul   Milan   Mexico City   Taipei

The paper used in this book meets the EPA standards for recycled fiber.

ISBN 0-201-40736-1
1 2 3 4 5 6 7 8 9-CRW-9796959493
First Printing, November 1993

# Contents

Chapter 3     **Writing Scripting Additions**     85

# Figures, Tables, and Listings

# About This Guide

The *AppleScript Scripting Additions Guide: English Dialect* describes the scripting additions that accompany the AppleScript English dialect of the AppleScript language. Scripting additions are files that extend the capabilities of the AppleScript language by providing additional commands you can use in scripts.

## Audience

This guide is for anyone who wants to write new scripts or modify existing scripts. It also provides some basic information for Macintosh software developers who want to write scripting additions.

Before using this guide, you should read *Getting Started With AppleScript* to learn what hardware and software you need to use AppleScript; how to install AppleScript; and how to run, record, and edit scripts. You should also be familiar with the *AppleScript Language Guide: English Dialect* (referred to throughout the rest of this book as the *AppleScript Language Guide*), which describes the English dialect of the AppleScript scripting language.

Macintosh software developers who want to write scripting additions should also refer to *Inside Macintosh: Interapplication Communication*.

## Organization of This Guide

This guide contains these chapters:

- Chapter 1, "Introduction to Scripting Additions," introduces scripting additions and the use of their commands.
- Chapter 2, "Scripting Addition Commands," describes the commands provided by the standard scripting additions that come with AppleScript.
- Chapter 3, "Writing Scripting Additions," provides information for programmers who wish to write scripting additions.

At the end of the guide are one appendix and an index.

- The appendix, "Scripting Additions at a Glance," summarizes the commands defined by the standard scripting additions.

# Sample Applications and Scripts

A sample application, the Scriptable Text Editor, is included with AppleScript. The Scriptable Text Editor is scriptable; that is, it understands scripts written in the AppleScript language. It also supports recording of scripts: when you use the Record button in the Script Editor (the application you use to write and modify scripts), the actions you perform in the Scriptable Text Editor generate AppleScript statements for performing those actions. Scripts for performing tasks in the Scriptable Text Editor are used as examples throughout this guide.

# For More Information

## Getting Started

See the companion book *Getting Started With AppleScript* to learn what hardware and software you need to use AppleScript; how to install AppleScript; and how to run, record, and edit scripts.

## AppleScript Language

See the companion book *AppleScript Language Guide* for complete information about the commands and other terms provided by the English dialect of the AppleScript scripting language and by the Scriptable Text Editor application.

## Other AppleScript Dialects

A *dialect* is a version of the AppleScript language that resembles a particular human language or a programming language. Each AppleScript dialect has a corresponding set of standard scripting additions for that dialect. This guide describes the terms defined by the standard scripting additions that come with the AppleScript English dialect. Scripting additions intended for use with other dialects work the same way but define terms and syntax appropriate for those dialects.

## Information for Programmers

If you are an experienced programmer and you want to write your own scripting additions, you should be thoroughly familiar with the Apple Event Manager, Apple event terminology resources, and the standard suites of Apple events. For information about the Apple Event Manager and Apple event terminology resources, see *Inside Macintosh: Interapplication Communication.* For definitions of the standard suites, see the *Apple Event Registry: Standard Suites.*

# Conventions Used in This Guide

Words and sample scripts in `monospaced font` are AppleScript language elements that must be typed exactly as shown.

Here are some additional conventions used in syntax descriptions:

`language element`

Plain computer font indicates an element that you must type exactly as shown. If there are special symbols (for example, + or &), you must also type them exactly as shown.

*placeholder*

Italic text indicates a placeholder that you must replace with an appropriate value. (In some programming languages, placeholders are called nonterminals.)

[ optional ]

Brackets indicate that the enclosed language element or elements are optional.

( a group )

Parentheses group together elements. If parentheses are part of the syntax, they are shown in bold.

[ optional ] **. . .**

Three ellipsis points (. . .) after a group defined by brackets indicate that you can repeat the group of elements within brackets 0 or more times.

( a group ) . . .    Three ellipsis points (. . .) after a group defined by parentheses indicate that you can repeat the group of elements within parentheses one or more times.

a | b | c    Vertical bars separate elements in a group from which you must choose a single element. The elements are often grouped within parentheses or brackets.

# CHAPTER 1

# Introduction to Scripting Additions

Scripting additions are files that extend the capabilities of the AppleScript language by providing additional commands or coercions you can use in scripts. They are similar to XCMDs and XFCNs in HyperTalk.

This chapter describes how to install scripting additions and briefly describes how scripting addition commands work. For more information about the differences between scripting addition commands, application commands, AppleScript commands, and user-defined commands, see Chapter 4, "Commands," of the *AppleScript Language Guide*.

## Installing Scripting Additions

When you install AppleScript using the Installer as described in *Getting Started With AppleScript*, the Installer creates a folder in the Extensions folder (which is located inside the System Folder for your computer) called Scripting Additions and copies a number of scripting addition files into that folder. The file type of a scripting addition (displayed in the Get Info window) is "AppleScript document."

Figure 1-1 shows a scripting addition icon. For a list of the scripting additions installed with AppleScript and the commands they provide, see Table 2-1 on page 6.

**Figure 1-1**     A scripting addition icon

Beep

Each scripting addition file contains one or more command handlers. If a scripting addition file is located in the Scripting Additions folder (in the Extensions folder of the System Folder), the command handlers it provides are available for use by any script whose target is an application on that computer.

Some scripting additions also define object classes for records returned by their commands. However, scripting addition commands do not normally act on objects defined by individual applications.

The scripting addition commands Activate, Log, Start Log, and Stop Log are part of the AppleScript extension and do not have separate files in the Scripting Additions folder. With the exception of these commands, AppleScript recognizes scripting addition commands only if the corresponding scripting addition files are located in the Scripting Additions folder. If after installing AppleScript you receive additional scripting additions from Apple or another vendor, you must copy them into the Scripting Additions folder before you can use their commands in scripts.

If you use a scripting addition command in a script and get an error message stating that the command is undefined, check to make sure the corresponding scripting addition is installed in the Scripting Additions folder.

# Sending Scripting Addition Commands

Like the target of an application command, the target of a scripting addition command is always an application object or a script object. If the script doesn't explicitly specify the target with a Tell statement, AppleScript sends the command to the default target application, which is usually the application running the script (for example, the Script Editor).

A scripting addition command performs its action only after the command has been received by a target application. Unlike application commands, scripting addition commands always work the same way regardless of the application to which they are sent.

For example, the scripting addition command Display Dialog displays a dialog box that can include text, one or more buttons, an icon, and a field in which the user can type text. In the script that follows, the target of the Display Dialog command is the Scriptable Text Editor application. When the script runs, the

Scriptable Text Editor becomes the frontmost application (that is, its menus become visible and its windows become the frontmost windows on the screen) and passes the command to the scripting addition's handler for the Display Dialog command, which displays the dialog box.

```
tell application "Scriptable Text Editor"
    display dialog "What's your name?" default answer ""
end tell
```

In the next example, the Display Dialog command is not enclosed in a Tell statement, nor does it have a direct parameter, so its target is the Script Editor (or whatever application runs the script). When you run the script, the Script Editor passes the command to the scripting addition's handler for the Display Dialog command, which displays the dialog box in the Script Editor's layer (that is, in front of any other Script Editor windows that may be open) while the Script Editor is still the active application.

```
set theCount to number of words in front document of ¬
    app "Scriptable Text Editor"
if theCount > 500 then
    display dialog "You have exceeded your word limit."
end
```

You can send scripting addition commands to a target on any remote computer whose Scripting Additions folder contains the appropriate scripting addition file. This is true no matter which scripting additions are available to the computer from which you are sending the command. For example, you can send the Display Dialog command to any application on a remote computer whose Scripting Additions folder contains the Display Dialog scripting addition, even if the Scripting Additions folder on your computer doesn't contain that file.

Each scripting addition that contains command handlers has its own dictionary, which lists the reserved words—including the command names, parameter labels, and in some cases object names—used to invoke the commands supported by the scripting addition. If a scripting addition dictionary includes words that are also part of an application dictionary, then you cannot use those words within Tell statements to that application.

For example, the Offset command provided by the String Commands scripting addition reports the offset, in characters, of a string within another string. Offset is also a property of several Scriptable Text Editor objects and is thus a word in the Scriptable Text Editor dictionary. Therefore, you cannot use Offset as a scripting addition command within Tell statements to the Scriptable Text Editor. If you do, you'll get a syntax error, because the Scriptable Text Editor treats the word Offset as a property of a text object.

If you specify a script object as the target of a scripting addition command, the script object either handles the command itself (potentially modifying it) or uses a Continue statement to pass the command to the default target application. For more information about scripting addition commands, script objects, and the Continue statement, see Chapter 9, "Script Objects," of the *AppleScript Language Guide*.

# Scripting Addition Commands

This chapter describes what the standard AppleScript scripting addition commands do and how to use them in scripts. The first two sections summarize the standard scripting addition files and the commands they provide. The last section describes in more detail how to use the commands provided by the Read/Write scripting addition, whose commands are usually used together.

## Scripting Addition Files

The standard scripting addition files are copied into the Scripting Additions folder (located in the Extensions folder in the System Folder) when you install AppleScript according to the instructions in *Getting Started With AppleScript.* Each file provides one or more commands. Table 2-1 summarizes the commands provided by the standard scripting additions.

Each scripting addition that provides commands includes its own dictionary of the commands and object classes it defines. You can open a scripting addition's dictionary in much the same way you open an application's dictionary—by selecting the scripting addition's icon in the Scripting Additions folder, dragging the icon over the Script Editor's icon, and releasing the mouse button.

For information about commands provided by scripting additions other than those described in this manual, see the documentation for those scripting additions. For information about using command definitions and for definitions of AppleScript commands and standard application commands, see the *AppleScript Language Guide.*

**Table 2-1**      Scripting addition commands described in this guide

| Name of scripting addition file | Name of command | Description of command |
|---|---|---|
| Not a separate file; part of AppleScript extension | Activate | Activates an application. |
| | Log | Places a string between comment characters in the Script Editor's Event Log Window. |
| | Start Log | Turns logging on in the Script Editor's Event Log window. |
| | Stop Log | Turns logging off in the Script Editor's Event Log window. |
| Beep | Beep | Plays the alert sound. |
| Choose Application | Choose Application | Allows the user to choose a running application from a dialog box. |
| Choose File | Choose File | Allows the user to choose a file from a dialog box. |
| | Choose Folder | Allows the user to choose a folder or volume from a dialog box. |
| Current Date | Current Date | Returns a date value that represents the current time and date. |
| Display Dialog | Display Dialog | Displays a dialog box. |
| File Commands | Info For | Gets information for a file or folder. |
| | List Disks | Returns a list of currently mounted disks. |
| | List Folder | Lists the contents of a specified folder. |
| | Path To | Returns full pathname to specified folder or application. |

*continued*

**Table 2-1**    Scripting addition commands described in this guide  (continued)

| Name of scripting addition file | Name of command | Description of command |
|---|---|---|
| Load Script | Load Script | Loads a compiled script into the current script as a script object. |
| New File | New File | Allows a user to create a new file. |
| Numerics | Random Number | Generates a random number. |
|  | Round | Rounds a number to the nearest integer. |
| Read/Write Commands | Close Access | Closes a file opened with Open for Access. |
|  | Get EOF | Returns the offset, in bytes, of the end of a specified file from the beginning of the file. |
|  | Open for Access | Opens a file for reading or writing using Read or Write commands. |
|  | Read | Reads data from file previously opened with Open for Access command, or opens file for access, reads data, and closes file. |
|  | Set EOF | Sets the end of a specified file. |
|  | Write | Writes data to file previously opened with Open for Access command, or opens file for access, writes data, and closes file. |
| Run Script | Run Script | Runs a specified script. |
| Scripting Components | Scripting Components | Returns a list of the scripting components currently available. |
| Store Script | Store Script | Stores a specified script object in a specified file. |

*continued*

**Table 2-1**    Scripting addition commands described in this guide  (continued)

| Name of scripting addition file | Name of command | Description of command |
| --- | --- | --- |
| String Commands | ASCII Character | Converts a number to its ASCII equivalent. |
| | ASCII Number | Returns the ASCII number of a character. |
| | Offset | Determines the offset of a string within another string. |
| Time to GMT | Time to GMT | Returns the difference, in seconds, between the current time and Greenwich mean time. |

# Command Definitions

The sections that follow are in alphabetical order by command name and provide definitions for all the standard scripting addition commands. For information about using command definitions, see Chapter 4, "Commands," of the *AppleScript Language Guide.*

## Activate

The Activate command brings an application to the front (that is, its window becomes the frontmost window on the desktop). If the application is on the local computer, AppleScript opens the application if it is not already running. If the application is on a remote computer, it must be running already.

Unlike most other scripting additions, the Activate command is built into the AppleScript extension. It does not have a separate file in the Scripting Additions folder.

**SYNTAX**

activate *referenceToApplication*

**PARAMETER**

*referenceToApplication*

A reference of the form application *nameString* (see "Notes").
*Class:* Reference

**RESULT**

None

**EXAMPLES**

```
set x to application "Scriptable Text Editor"
activate x

activate application ¬
   "Mac HD:Applications:Scriptable Text Editor"

tell application "Scriptable Text Editor"
   activate
end tell

tell application "Scriptable Text Editor" to activate
```

**NOTES**

The way you specify the name (*nameString*) of the application you want to activate depends on whether the application is on a local or remote computer.

To specify an application on the local computer, use a string of the form "*Disk*:*Folder1*:*Folder2*: . . . :*ApplicationName*". You can also specify a string with only an application name ("*ApplicationName*"). In this case, AppleScript attempts to find the application in the current directory.

To specify an application on a remote computer, you must use a string that consists of the name of the application as it would be listed in the Application menu ("*ApplicationName*"), and you must also specify the name of the computer and if necessary the zone in which the computer is located. The application must be running. The Activate command does not launch applications on remote machines.

For more information about references to applications, see Chapter 5, "Objects and References," of the *AppleScript Language Guide*.

**ERRORS**

| Error number | Error message |
|---|---|
| –600 | Application isn't running. |
| –606 | Application is background-only. |

# ASCII Character

The ASCII Character command returns the ASCII character associated with a specified number. It is one of several commands provided by the String Commands scripting addition.

**SYNTAX**

```
ASCII character integer
```

**PARAMETER**

*integer*　　　　An expression that evaluates to an integer between 1 and 255. *Class:* Integer

**RESULT**

The character that corresponds to the specified ASCII number.

**EXAMPLES**

```
ASCII character 100
--result: "d"

ASCII character 101
--result: "e"
```

**ERRORS**

| Error number | Error message |
|---|---|
| –108 | Out of memory. |
| –1700 | Can't make some data into the expected type. |
| –1701 | Some parameter is missing for <commandName>. |
| –1704 | Some parameter was invalid. |
| –1705 | Operation involving a list item failed. |
| –1718 | Reply has not yet arrived. |
| –1720 | Invalid range. |

# ASCII Number

The ASCII Number command returns the ASCII number associated with a specified character. It is one of several commands provided by the String Commands scripting addition.

**SYNTAX**

```
ASCII number string
```

**PARAMETER**

*string*  An ASCII character.
*Class:* String

**RESULT**

The ASCII number that corresponds to the specified character.

**EXAMPLES**

```
ASCII number "d"
--result: 100

ASCII number "e"
--result: 101
```

**ERRORS**

| Error number | Error message |
| --- | --- |
| –108 | Out of memory. |
| –1700 | Can't make some data into the expected type. |
| –1701 | Some parameter is missing for <commandName>. |
| –1704 | Some parameter was invalid. |
| –1705 | Operation involving a list item failed. |
| –1715 | Some parameter wasn't understood. |
| –1718 | Reply has not yet arrived. |
| –1720 | Invalid range. |

## Beep

The Beep command plays the alert sound for the Macintosh. It is the only command provided by the Beep scripting addition.

**SYNTAX**

beep  [  *numberOfBeeps*  ]

**PARAMETER**

*numberOfBeeps*

The number of times to play the alert sound. If you omit *numberOfBeeps*, the alert sound is played once.
*Class:* Integer
*Default Value:* 1

**RESULT**

None

**EXAMPLES**

beep
beep  3

**NOTES**

The user can cancel a Beep command—for example, if the value of the *numberOfBeeps* parameter is large—by typing Command-period or pressing the Esc key.

## Choose Application

The Choose Application command allows the user to choose a running application from a dialog box like the one shown in Figure 2-1.

**Figure 2-1**    A Choose Application dialog box

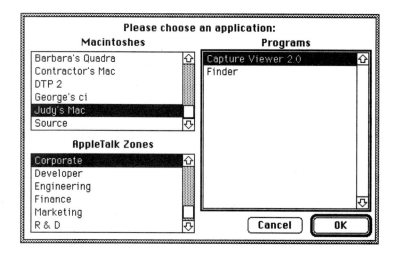

The dialog box displays applications on the current computer and on any computer connected to the same network.

Choose Application is the only command provided by the Choose Application scripting addition.

SYNTAX

```
choose application [ with prompt promptString ] ¬
    [ application label appListLabel ]
```

**PARAMETERS**

*promptString*     The prompt to be displayed in the dialog box. The prompt can be up to 255 characters long, but the standard dialog box has room for only about 50 characters. If you omit the `with prompt` parameter, the string `"Choose a program to link to:"` is displayed.
*Class:* String
*Default Value:* `"Choose a program to link to:"`

*appListLabel*     The label above the list of applications displayed in the dialog box. The label can be up to 255 characters long, but the standard dialog box has room for only about 25 characters. If you omit the `application label` parameter, the string `"Programs"` is displayed.
*Class:* String
*Default Value:* `"Programs"`

**RESULT**

A reference to the application specified by the user.

**EXAMPLES**

```
choose application with prompt "Choose a spelling checker:"

tell (choose application with prompt ¬
   "Choose a scriptable text editor:")
      --other statements
end tell
```

**NOTES**

If the user chooses the Cancel button, Display Dialog returns error –128. If you want your script to continue after the user clicks Cancel, you must include an error handler. For information about Tell statements and error handlers, see Chapter 8, "Handlers," of the *AppleScript Language Guide*.

**ERRORS**

| Error number | Error message |
|---|---|
| –108 | Out of memory. |
| –128 | User canceled. |

# Choose File

The Choose File command displays a dialog box like the one in Figure 2-2 to allow the user to choose a file.

Figure 2-2    A Choose File dialog box

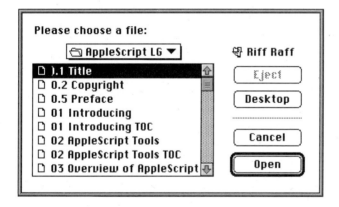

The Choose File command is one of two commands provided by the Choose File scripting addition.

**SYNTAX**

choose file [ with prompt *promptString* ] [ of type *listOfTypes* ]

**PARAMETERS**

*promptString*   The prompt to be displayed in the dialog box. The prompt can be up to 255 characters long, but the standard dialog box has room for only about 40 characters. If you omit the `with prompt` parameter, no prompt is displayed.
*Class:* String
*Default Value:* (no prompt)

*listOfTypes*   A list of the file types of the files to be displayed in the dialog box. Each string is a four-character code for the file type, such as `"TEXT"`, `"APPL"`, `"PICT"`, or `"PNTG"`. If you omit the `of type` parameter, all files are displayed.
*Class:* List of strings; each string is a four-letter code
*Default Value:* (all file types displayed)

**RESULT**

A reference of the form `file "`*Disk*`:`*Folder1*`:`*Folder2*`:`...`:`*Filename*`"` for the file specified by the user, if any.

**EXAMPLE**

```
choose file with prompt "Please choose a file:" of type ¬
    {"TEXT", "APPL"}
open result
```

**NOTES**

If the user clicks Cancel in the Choose File dialog box, AppleScript returns error number –128. If you want your script to continue after the user clicks Cancel, you must include an error handler. For information about Try statements and error handlers, see Chapter 7, "Control Statements," of the *AppleScript Language Guide.*

**ERRORS**

| Error number | Error message |
|---|---|
| –108 | Out of memory. |
| –128 | User canceled. |

## Choose Folder

The Choose Folder command displays a dialog box like the one in Figure 2-3 to allow the user to choose a directory (that is, a folder, a volume, or the desktop).

**Figure 2-3**     A Choose Folder dialog box

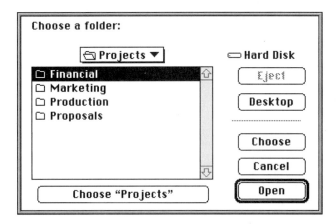

The Choose Folder command is one of two commands provided by the Choose File scripting addition.

**SYNTAX**

choose folder [ with prompt *promptString* ]


**PARAMETERS**

*promptString*     The prompt that appears in the dialog box. The prompt can be up to 255 characters long, but the standard dialog box has room for only about 80 characters. If you omit the `with prompt` parameter, the string `"Choose a folder:"` is displayed.
*Class:* String
*Default Value:* `"Choose a folder:"`

**RESULT**

A reference of the form `file` "*Disk:Folder1:Folder2:...:Foldername*" for the
directory specified by the user, if any.

**EXAMPLE**

```
choose folder with prompt "Choose a folder or volume:"
```

**NOTES**

If the user clicks Cancel in the Choose Folder dialog box, AppleScript returns
error number –128. If you want your script to continue after the user clicks
Cancel, you must include an error handler. For information about Try
statements and error handlers, see Chapter 7, "Control Statements," in the
*AppleScript Language Guide.*

**ERRORS**

| Error number | Error message |
|---|---|
| –108 | Out of memory. |
| –128 | User canceled. |

## Close Access

The Close Access command closes a file opened with the Open for Access
command. It is one of several commands provided by the Read/Write
Commands scripting addition. For more information about these commands,
see "Using Read/Write Commands," which begins on page 70.

**SYNTAX**

```
close access referenceToFile
```

**PARAMETER**

*referenceToFile* A reference of the form `file` *nameString* or `alias` *nameString*, or a file reference number returned by a previous call to the Open for Access command (see "Notes").
*Class:* Reference or integer

**RESULT**

None

**EXAMPLES**

This example closes the file named To Donald in the specified location if it was previously opened with the Open for Access command.

```
tell application "Scriptable Text Editor"
    close access file "Hard Disk:Letters:To Donald"
end tell
```

The next example closes the file associated with the file reference number if the value of `myFileRefNumber` is a file reference number previously obtained with the Open for Access command.

```
tell application "Scriptable Text Editor"
    close access myFileRefNumber
end tell
```

**NOTES**

To specify the name (*nameString*) of a file, use a string of the form "*Disk*:*Folder1*: *Folder2*:....:*Filename*" as described in Chapter 5, "Objects and References," of the *AppleScript Language Guide.* If you specify only the name of the file (*Filename*) instead of its entire pathname, AppleScript attempts to find the file in the current directory.

If you specify a reference to a file or an alias, the Close Access command attempts to match the reference with a file previously opened with the Open for Access command. If a match is found, Close Access closes the file. If no match is found, Close Access returns error number –43.

If you specify a file reference number previously obtained with the Open for Access command, Close Access closes the file immediately.

**ERRORS**

| Error number | Error message |
|---|---|
| –35 | Disk <name> wasn't found. |
| –38 | File <name> wasn't open. |
| –43 | File <name> wasn't found. |
| –50 | Parameter error. |

# Current Date

The Current Date command returns a date value that represents the current time, day, and date. It is the only command provided by the Current Date scripting addition.

**SYNTAX**

```
current date
```

**RESULT**

A date value.

**EXAMPLES**

```
set timeOfTransfer to current date
get timeOfTransfer

if (current date) = ¬
    date "Saturday, January 23, 1993 12:00:00 AM" then
        print the front window
else
    return "The date is not " & ¬
        "Saturday, January 23, 1993 12:00:00 AM"
end if
```

**ERRORS**

| Error number | Error message |
| --- | --- |
| –108 | Out of memory. |
| –1700 | Can't make some data into the expected type. |
| –1701 | Some parameter is missing for <commandName>. |
| –1704 | Some parameter was invalid. |
| –1705 | Operation involving a list item failed. |
| –1718 | Reply has not yet arrived. |

## Display Dialog

The Display Dialog command displays a dialog box like the one shown in Figure 2-4. The dialog box contains a string and one or more buttons, such as Yes and No, or OK and Cancel. The dialog box may also contain an icon and a field in which the user can enter text.

The Display Dialog command is the only command provided by the Display Dialog scripting addition.

**Figure 2-4**    A Display Dialog dialog box

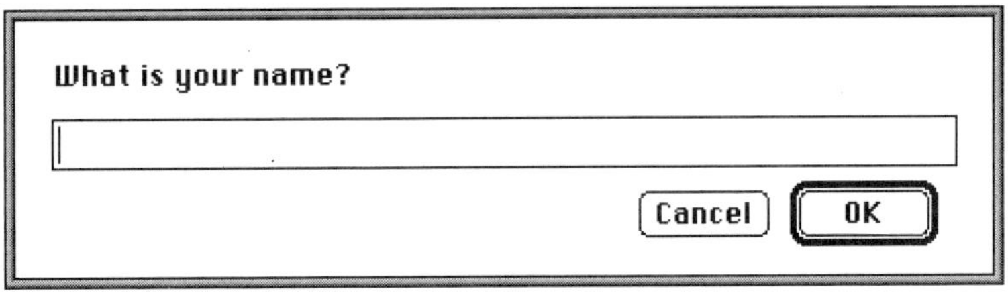

**SYNTAX**

```
display dialog questionString                                  ¬
    [ default answer answerString ]                            ¬
    [ buttons buttonList]                                      ¬
    [ default button buttonNumberOrName ]                      ¬
    [ with icon iconNumberOrName ]
```

**PARAMETERS**

*questionString*

> The string displayed in the dialog box. The string can be up to 255 characters long.
> *Class:* String

*answerString*

> The default string provided in a text field that the user can edit. The string can be up to 255 characters long. If you omit the `default answer` parameter, the dialog box does not include an editable text field. If you specify an empty string (" "), the dialog box has an editable text field with no default answer.
> *Class:* String

*buttonList*

> The list of buttons that appear in the dialog box. Each item in the list is a string containing the text that appears in the button. The first string in the list is the string for the leftmost button, the second string is the string for the next button, and so on. You can specify up to three buttons. If you omit the `buttons` parameter, the dialog contains two buttons: Cancel and OK.
> *Class:* List of strings

*buttonNumberOrName*

> The default button. You can specify the default button with a
> string (the string provided for the button in *buttonList*) or with
> an integer (which specifies the position of the button in the
> *buttonList* list; 1 specifies the first button from the left, 2 specifies
> the second button from the left, and so on).
> *Class:* String or integer

*iconNumberOrName*

> The icon to be included in the dialog box. This can be either a
> string that specifies the name of an `'ICON'` resource or an
> integer that specifies the number of the resource (see "Notes").
> *Class:* String

**RESULT**

A record of object class Reply (defined by the Display Dialog scripting
addition) that contains the following properties:

`button returned`

> The text of the button the user pressed to close the dialog box.
> *Class:* String

`text returned`

> The text from the editable text field in the dialog box. If the
> dialog does not include an editable text field, no string is
> returned. If there is no text in the field, the value is the empty
> string (`" "`).
> *Class:* String

**EXAMPLE**

The following example uses the Display Dialog command to prompt the user
for a password.

```
set prompt to "Please enter password:"
repeat with i from 1 to 4
    set dialogResult to display dialog prompt ¬
        buttons {"I give up", "OK"} default button 2 ¬
        default answer  "Joe User" with icon 1
    if button returned of dialogResult = "I give up" then
        error number -128 --user canceled
    else
        if text returned of dialogResult = "magic" then
            exit
        else
            if i < 3 then
                set prompt to "Password was incorrect.  Try " ¬
                    & i + 1
            else
                set prompt to ¬
                    "Password was incorrect.  Last Chance!"
            end if
        end if
    end if
end repeat
```

NOTES

The size of the dialog box is determined by the lengths of the question and answer strings.

As an alternative to the Cancel button, the user can press Command-period or the Esc key to cancel a dialog box displayed by the Display Dialog command.

A dialog box can include an icon stored in the script file, the current application (as specified by a Tell statement), or the System file. If there is an icon with the specified name or number in the script file, it is used; otherwise, AppleScript checks the current application; finally, if the specified icon is not found in either the script file or the current application, AppleScript checks the System file. If you are using a system that provides Color QuickDraw and the specified icon is available as a color icon, the color icon is displayed. To add icons to a script or application file, use a resource tool such as ResEdit.

The System file provides three standard icons to warn the user about problems. These icons, illustrated in Figure 2-5, have the following meanings:

■ Stop (icon number 0). Use this icon to call attention to a serious problem that requires the user to choose from alternative courses of action.

■ Note (icon number 1). Use this icon to provide information about a situation that has no drastic effects. The user usually responds by pressing the OK button.

■ Caution (icon number 2). Use this icon to call attention to an operation that may have undesirable results if allowed to continue. You normally give the user a choice to continue or not.

**Figure 2-5**     Alert icons

0            1            2

To use these icons, refer to them by number. For example, this script displays the caution icon, the string, and the default OK and Cancel buttons.

```
display dialog "Your fuselage is melting. Eject now?" ¬
     with icon 2
```

**ERRORS**

| Error number | Error message |
|---|---|
| −108 | Out of memory. |
| −128 | User canceled. |
| −192 | A resource wasn't found. |
| −1712 | AppleEvent timed out. |

# Get EOF

The Get EOF command returns an integer that indicates the offset, in bytes, of the end of a specified file from the beginning of the file. It is one of several commands provided by the Read/Write Commands scripting addition. For more information about these commands, see "Using Read/Write Commands," which begins on page 70.

### SYNTAX

get eof *referenceToFile*

### PARAMETER

*referenceToFile*

A reference of the form file *nameString* or alias *nameString*, or a file reference number returned by a previous call to the Open for Access command (see "Notes").
*Class:* Reference or integer

### RESULT

If the command is successful, it returns an integer indicating the offset of the end of the specified file.

### EXAMPLE

get eof file "Hard Disk:Status Reports:Weekly Report"

### NOTES

To specify the name (*nameString*) of a file, use a string of the form "*Disk*:*Folder1*: *Folder2*:....:*Filename*" as described in Chapter 5, "Objects and References," of the *AppleScript Language Guide*. If you specify only the name of the file (*Filename*) instead of its entire pathname, AppleScript attempts to find the file in the current directory.

If you specify a reference to a file or an alias, the Get EOF command attempts to match the reference with a file previously opened with the Open for Access command. (It doesn't matter whether the file was opened with read-only permission or with write permission.) If a match is found, Get EOF returns an integer indicating the offset of the end of the file. If no match is found, Get EOF opens the file, gets the end of the file, then closes the file.

If you specify a file reference number previously obtained with the Open for Access command, the Get EOF command returns a result immediately.

**ERRORS**

| Error number | Error message |
|---|---|
| –38 | File <<name>> wasn't open. |
| –50 | Parameter error. |
| –51 | File reference number error. |

# Info For

The Info For command returns a record that contains information about a specified file or folder. The Info For command is one of several commands provided by the File Commands scripting addition.

**SYNTAX**

info for *referenceToFile*

**PARAMETER**

*referenceToFile*

A reference of the form file *nameString* or alias *nameString*.
*Class:* Reference

**RESULT**

A record of object class File Info (defined by the File Commands scripting addition) that contains the following properties:

name
: Name of file or folder.
  *Class:* String

creation date
: Date and time the file or folder was first created.
  *Class:* Date

modification date
: Date and time the file or folder was last modified.
  *Class:* Date

icon position
: Location of the upper-left corner of the file or folder's icon.
  *Class:* Point (defined by the QuickDraw suite as a two-item list of integers for horizontal and vertical coordinates)

visible
: A value that indicates whether the file or folder's icon is visible on the desktop (true) or not (false).
  *Class:* Boolean
  *Modifiable?* No

size
: The size of the file or folder in bytes.
  *Class:* Integer
  *Modifiable?* No

folder
: A value that indicates whether the object described by the File Info record is a folder (true) or a file (false).
  *Class:* Boolean
  *Modifiable?* No

alias
: Indicates whether the file is an alias (true) or not (false).
  *Class:* Boolean
  *Modifiable?* No

folder window
: Four integers that specify the bounding rectangle of the folder window. Returned for folders only.
  *Class:* Bounding rectangle (a list of four integers)
  *Modifiable?* No

locked       Indicates whether the file or folder is locked (true) or unlocked (false).
*Class:* Boolean
*Modifiable?* No

file creator
Four-character creator code of the file. Returned for files only.
*Class:* String
*Modifiable?* No

file type     Four-character code for the file type of the file. Returned for files only.
*Class:* String
*Modifiable?* No

short version
The file's short version, if any. Returned for files only.
*Class:* String
*Modifiable?* No

long version
The file's long version, if any. Returned for files only.
*Class:* String
*Modifiable?* No

default application
The default application for a nonapplication file (for example, TeachText). Used with nonapplication files only.
*Class:* Alias
*Modifiable?* No

**EXAMPLES**

This example returns the entire File Info record for Scriptable Text Editor.

```
info for file "Hard Disk:Scriptable Text Editor"
--result: {name:"Scriptable Text Editor", creation
date:date "Tuesday, April 6, 1993 11:30:00 AM",
modification date:date "Tuesday, April 6, 1993 11:30:00
AM", icon position:{20, 349}, visible:true, size:88988,
folder:false, alias:false, locked:false, file
creator:"quil", file type:"APPL", short version:"1.1",
long version:"1.1, Copyright © Apple Computer, Inc.
1991-93"}
```

This example returns just the file type for Scriptable Text Editor.

```
set x to info for ¬
    file "Turing's World:Scriptable Text Editor"
x's file type
--result: "APPL"
```

This example displays a dialog box if the Scriptable Text Editor isn't locked.

```
if locked of ¬
    (info for file "Hard Disk:Scriptable Text Editor") ¬
    is false then
        display dialog "Scriptable Text Editor is not locked."
end if
```

**NOTES**

To specify the name (*nameString*) of a file, use a string of the form "*Disk* : *Folder1* : *Folder2* : . . . : *Filename*" as described in Chapter 5, "Objects and References," of the *AppleScript Language Guide.* If you specify only the name of the file (*Filename*) instead of its entire pathname, AppleScript attempts to find the file in the current directory.

**ERRORS**

| Error number | Error message |
|---|---|
| –35 | Disk <name> wasn't found. |
| –37 | Bad name for file. |
| –43 | File <name> wasn't found. |
| –50 | Parameter error. |
| –108 | Out of memory. |
| –120 | Folder <name> wasn't found. |
| –1700 | Can't make some data into the expected type. |
| –1701 | Some parameter is missing for <commandName>. |
| –1704 | Some parameter was invalid. |
| –1705 | Operation involving a list item failed. |
| –1718 | Reply has not yet arrived. |

# List Disks

The List Disks command returns a list containing the names of every mounted volume, including CD-ROMs, floppy disks, AppleShare volumes, and so on. List Disks is one of several commands provided by the File Commands scripting addition.

**SYNTAX**

```
list disks
```

**RESULT**

The result is a list of strings.

**EXAMPLE**

```
list disks
--result: {"My Disk", "Our Server", "Joe's Floppy"}
```

**ERROR**

| Error number | Error message |
|---|---|
| –35 | Disk <name> wasn't found. |
| –50 | Parameter error. |
| –108 | Out of memory. |
| –1703 | Some data was the wrong type. |
| –1704 | Some parameter was invalid. |
| –1705 | Operation involving a list item failed. |
| –1719 | Can't get <reference>. Invalid index. |

## List Folder

The List Folder command returns a list of every file and folder in a specified folder or volume. List Folder is one of several commands provided by the File Commands scripting addition.

**SYNTAX**

```
list folder referenceToFolder
```

**PARAMETER**

*referenceToFolder*
>A reference of the form `file` *nameString*, `alias` *nameString*, or `folder` *nameString* (see "Notes").
>*Class:* Reference or string

**RESULT**

A list of strings.

**EXAMPLE**

```
list folder "My Disk:"
--result: {"Letters", "Current", "Projects", "Aliases"}
```

**NOTES**

To specify the name (*nameString*) of a folder, use a string of the form "*Disk*:*Folder1*:*Folder2*:...:*FolderName*" as described in Chapter 5, "Objects and References," of the *AppleScript Language Guide.* If you specify only the name of the folder (*FolderName*) instead of its entire pathname, AppleScript attempts to find the folder in the current directory.

**ERRORS**

| Error number | Error message |
|---|---|
| –35 | Disk <name> wasn't found. |
| –37 | Bad name for file. |
| –43 | File <name> wasn't found. |
| –50 | Parameter error. |
| –108 | Out of memory. |
| –120 | Folder <name> wasn't found. |
| –1700 | Can't make some data into the expected type. |
| –1701 | Some parameter is missing for <commandName>. |
| –1703 | Some data was the wrong type. |
| –1704 | Some parameter was invalid. |
| –1705 | Operation involving a list item failed. |
| –1718 | Reply has not yet arrived. |
| –1719 | Can't get <reference>. Invalid index. |

# Load Script

The Load Script command loads a compiled script into the current script as a script object. A script object is a user-defined object that is treated as a value by AppleScript. Script objects are described in Chapter 9, "Script Objects," of the *AppleScript Language Guide*.

Load Script is the only command provided by the Load Script scripting addition.

**SYNTAX**

```
load script referenceToFile
```

PARAMETER

*referenceToFile* A reference of the form `file` *nameString* or `alias` *nameString* (see "Notes"). The file must be a compiled script file or a script application file. It cannot be a text file.
*Class:* Reference

RESULT

A script object.

EXAMPLES

The following example loads a compiled script called Numeric Operations and stores the resulting script object in the variable `NumericLib`. The Tell statement shows how to call a subroutine contained in the script object.

```
load script file "MacHD:Scripts:Numeric Operations"
set NumericLib to result

tell NumericLib
    factorial(10)
end tell
```

NOTES

To specify the name (*nameString*) of a file, use a string of the form "*Disk* : *Folder1* : *Folder2* : . . . : *Filename*" as described in Chapter 5, "Objects and References," of the *AppleScript Language Guide*. If you specify only the name of the file (*Filename*) instead of its entire pathname, AppleScript attempts to find the file in the current directory.

For more information about using Load Script to save and load libraries of subroutines for use in multiple scripts, see Chapter 8, "Handlers," of the *AppleScript Language Guide*.

**ERRORS**

| Error number | Error message |
|---|---|
| –108 | Out of memory. |
| –192 | Bad name for file. |
| –1700 | Can't make some data into the expected type. |
| –1701 | Some parameter is missing for <commandName>. |
| –1703 | Some data was the wrong type. |
| –1704 | Some parameter was invalid. |
| –1705 | Operation involving a list item failed. |
| –1718 | Reply has not yet arrived. |

# Log

The Log command displays a specified string between comment characters (* and *) in the Script Editor's Event Log window. For more information about the Log Events window, see page 61.

Unlike most other scripting additions, the Log command is built into the AppleScript extension. It does not have a separate file in the Scripting Additions folder.

**SYNTAX**

log *stringToLog*

**PARAMETER**

*stringToLog*  An expression that evaluates to a string or to a value that can be coerced to a string. The resulting string is displayed in the Event Log window.
*Class:* String

**RESULT**

None

**EXAMPLE**

```
log "This string appears in the Log Events window"
```

After running the preceding script, this text appears in the Log Events window:

```
(* This string appears in the Log Events window" *)
```

**NOTES**

The Log command works even if logging has not been turned on with the Start Log command or has been turned off with the Stop Log command. If logging is turned off before the Log command is sent, it will still be turned off after the Log command is sent.

**ERROR**

| Error number | Error message |
| --- | --- |
| –1700 | Can't make some data into the expected type. |

## New File

The New File command displays a dialog box like the one in Figure 2-6 to allow the user to specify a filename and a location. New File does not create a new file; rather, it returns a reference to a file with the name and location specified by the user. You can store the reference in a variable and pass it to Open for Access (which in turn creates the file in the specified location) or to any other command for which you want to specify a file that doesn't yet exist.

New File is the only command provided by the New File scripting addition.

**Figure 2-6**     A New File dialog box

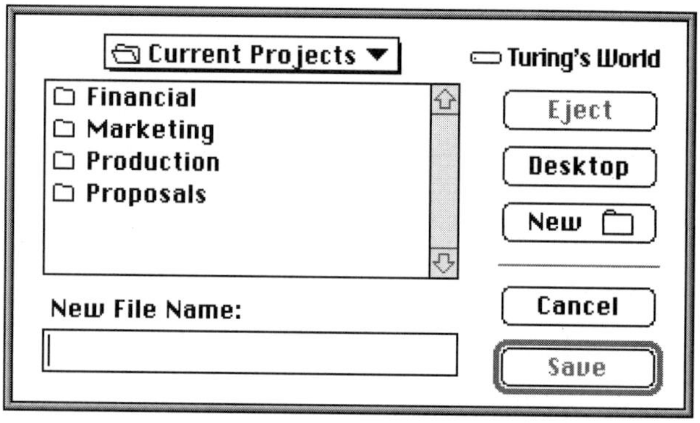

**SYNTAX**

new file [ with prompt *promptString* ] [ default name *defaultName* ]

**PARAMETERS**

*promptString*   The prompt that appears in the dialog box. The string you
             specify can be up to 255 characters long. If you omit the
             with prompt parameter, the prompt "New File Name"
             is displayed.
             *Class:* String
             *Default Value:* "New File Name"

*defaultName*    The default filename that appears in the dialog box. The string
             you specify can be up to 255 characters long. If you omit the
             default name parameter, no default filename is displayed.
             *Class:* String
             *Default Value:* (no default name)

**RESULT**

A reference of the form file "*Disk*:*Folder1*:*Folder2*:....:*Filename*" for the
filename and location specified by the user.

**EXAMPLES**

```
set x to new file
open for access x
```

**NOTES**

If the user chooses the Cancel button, New File returns error –128. If you want your script to continue after the user clicks Cancel, you must include an error handler. For information about Tell statements and error handlers, see Chapter 8, "Handlers," of the *AppleScript Language Guide*.

**ERRORS**

| Error number | Error message |
|---|---|
| –108 | Out of memory. |
| –128 | User canceled. |

# Offset

The Offset command returns the offset of a string within a string. For example, the offset of "freedom now" contained in "Yes, freedom now" is 6, because the contained string begins with the sixth character of the container. The offset of "Yes" in the string "Yes, freedom now" is 1, because it begins with the first character of the container string. The Offset command is case-sensitive.

Offset is one of several commands provided by the String Commands scripting addition.

**SYNTAX**

```
offset of stringToFind in stringToSearch
```

**PARAMETERS**

> *stringToFind*
>> The string to find in *stringToSearch*.
>> *Class:* String
>
> *stringToSearch*
>> A string containing *stringToFind*.
>> *Class:* String

**RESULT**

> The result is an integer that indicates the offset, in number of characters, of the first character of *stringToFind* from the beginning of *stringToSearch*. If *stringToFind* is not contained within *stringToSearch*, AppleScript returns the value 0.

**EXAMPLES**

```
offset of "yours" in "yours, mine, and ours"
--result: 1

offset of "mine" in "yours, mine, and ours"
--result: 8

offset of "this" in "yours, mine, and ours"
--result: 0

offset of "Mine" in "yours, mine, and ours"
--result: 0, due to case sensitivity
```

**NOTES**

> The Offset command compares strings character by character, as the Equals operator does, except that the Offset command is always case-sensitive, always considers diacritical marks, and is not affected by Considering or Ignoring statements.

| Error number | Error message |
|---|---|
| –50 | Parameter error. |
| –108 | Out of memory. |
| –1700 | Can't make some data into the expected type. |
| –1701 | Some parameter is missing for <commandName>. |
| –1704 | Some parameter was invalid. |
| –1705 | Operation involving a list item failed. |
| –1708 | <reference> doesn't understand the <commandName> message. |
| –1718 | Reply has not yet arrived. |

## Open for Access

The Open for Access command opens access to a file for reading or writing using the Read and Write commands. Opening a file for reading and writing is not the same as opening it with the Open command. The file is open only in the sense that AppleScript has access to it for reading and writing data; it doesn't appear in one of the target application's windows, and it doesn't even have to be one of the target application's files.

Open for Access is one of several commands provided by the Read/Write Commands scripting addition. For more information about these commands, see "Using Read/Write Commands," which begins on page 70.

```
open for access referenceToFile [ write permission Boolean ]
```

**PARAMETERS**

*referenceToFile*

A reference of the form `file` *nameString* or `alias` *nameString*. If you specify an alias, the file must already exist, because AppleScript must locate the file before running the script. If you specify a file that doesn't exist using the form `file` *nameString*, Open for Access creates a TeachText document of that name at the specified location and opens it for access.
*Class:* Reference

*Boolean*

An expression that evaluates to `true` or `false`. If it evaluates to `true`, AppleScript opens the file with read and write permission. If it evaluates to `false` or if this parameter is omitted entirely, AppleScript opens the file with read permission only. Note that the phrase `with write permission` is equivalent to the phrase `write permission true`; similarly, `without write permission` is equivalent to `write permission false`.
*Class:* Boolean

**RESULT**

File reference number.

**EXAMPLE**

This example opens the file named To Donald in the specified location for subsequent access with the Read command.

```
tell application "Scriptable Text Editor"
    open for access file "Hard Disk:Letters:To Donald"
end tell
```

The next example opens the file associated with the file reference number for subsequent access with the Read or Write command.

```
tell application "Scriptable Text Editor"
    open for access alias "Hard Disk:Aliases:To Donald" ¬
        with write permission
end tell
```

**NOTES**

To specify the name (*nameString*) of a file, use a string of the form "*Disk* : *Folder1* : *Folder2* : . . . : *Filename*" as described in Chapter 5, "Objects and References," of the *AppleScript Language Guide*. If you specify only the name of the file (*Filename*) instead of its entire pathname, AppleScript attempts to find the file in the current directory.

**ERRORS**

| Error number | Error message |
| --- | --- |
| –35 | Disk <name> wasn't found. |
| –37 | Bad name for file. |
| –42 | Too many files open. |
| –43 | File <name> wasn't found. |
| –44 | Disk <name> is write protected. |
| –49 | File <name> is already open. |
| –50 | Parameter error. |

# Path To

The Path To command allows you to get the pathname, in the form of either an alias or a string, of some of the standard folders on a startup disk. It also allows you to get the location on disk of the frontmost application.

Path To is one of several commands provided by the File Commands scripting addition.

**SYNTAX**

> path to *folderOrApplication* [ as *className* ]

**PARAMETERS**

> *folderOrApplication*
>> One of these constants:
>> apple menu
>> apple menu items
>> control panels
>> desktop
>> extensions
>> preferences
>> printmonitor
>> printmonitor documents
>> trash
>> startup items
>> system folder
>> temporary items
>> startup disk
>> frontmost application
>
> *className*  The class identifier string. If you omit this parameter, the pathname is returned as an alias.

**RESULT**

> An alias by default, or a string if you include the optional as string parameter.

**EXAMPLES**

```
path to control panels
--result: alias "Hard Disk:System Folder:Control Panels:"

tell application "Scriptable Text Editor"
   set x to path to it as string
end tell
--result: "Hard Disk:Scriptable Text Editor"
```

```
tell application "Scriptable Text Editor"
   activate
   tell application "HyperCard" to activate
   set x to path to frontmost application
end tell
return x
--result: alias "Hard Disk:Applications:HyperCard"
```

**NOTES**

The optional as parameter is useful if you send the Path To command to an application on a remote computer. If the pathname is returned as a string, you can use the form file *nameString* to identify the folder or application across the network, and Path To won't actually attempt to locate it until you run the script. If the pathname is returned as an alias and you use it to refer to the folder or application elsewhere in the script, Path To also attempts to locate the file whenever you modify the script and then attempt to check its syntax or save it, requiring appropriate access privileges and possibly a password each time.

**ERRORS**

| Error number | Error message |
| --- | --- |
| −50 | Parameter error. |
| −108 | Out of memory. |
| −1700 | Can't make some data into the expected type. |
| −1701 | Some parameter is missing for <commandName>. |
| −1704 | Some parameter was invalid. |
| −1705 | Operation involving a list item failed. |
| −1708 | <reference> doesn't understand the <commandName> message. |
| −1718 | Reply has not yet arrived. |

# Random Number

The Random Number command generates a random number. It is one of two commands provided by the Numerics scripting addition.

SYNTAX

```
random number                                        ¬
    [ numberToRandomize ]                            ¬
    [ from beginningNumber to endNumber ]            ¬
    [ with seed seedNumber ]
```

PARAMETERS

*numberToRandomize*

A number that specifies the upper limit of the range within which you want to generate a random number. If this number is a real value, the value returned is a real value; if this number is an integer value, the value returned is an integer.
*Class:* Real or integer

*beginningNumber*

A number that indicates the beginning of the range within which you want to generate a random number. If this number and *endNumber* are both integers, the value returned is an integer. If either this number or *endNumber* is a real value, the value returned is a real value.
*Class:* Real or integer

*endNumber*

A number that indicates the end of the range within which you want to generate a random number. If this number and *beginningNumber* are both integers, the value returned is an integer. If either this number or *beginningNumber* is a real value, the value returned is a real value.
*Class:* Real or integer

*seedNumber*

A number that specifies the number to use as the seed in generating a random number.
*Class:* Real or integer

**RESULT**

A random number within the specified limits. If no parameters are included,
Random Number returns a real value between 0.0 and 1.0.

**EXAMPLES**

```
display dialog "A random number between 0 and 1: " & ¬
    (random number)

display dialog ¬
    "A random integer between 1 and 10: " & ¬
    (random number from 1 to 10)

display dialog ¬
    "A random real value between 1 and 10.0 : " & ¬
    (random number from 1 to 10.0)

display dialog ¬
    "A random real value between -10.0 and 10 : " & ¬
    (random number from -10.0 to 10)

display dialog ¬
    "A random integer between 1 and 10, 12 as seed: " & ¬
    (random number from 1 to 10 with seed 12)
```

After the seed is set, subsequent numbers generated by the Random Number
command in the same script can be determined.

```
display dialog "This should be 9: " & ¬
    (random number from 1 to 10)
display dialog "This should be 1: " & ¬
    (random number from 1 to 10)
```

Reseeding with the value 0 causes the seed to be reset to a random value each time the command is called.

```
display dialog ¬
    "After reseeding with 0, a truly random number: " & ¬
    (random number from 1 to 10 with seed 0)
```

**ERRORS**

| Error number | Error message |
|---|---|
| –50 | Parameter error. |
| –108 | Out of memory. |
| –1700 | Can't make some data into the expected type. |
| –1701 | Some parameter is missing for <commandName>. |
| –1704 | Some parameter was invalid. |
| –1705 | Operation involving a list item failed. |
| –1708 | <reference> doesn't understand the <commandName> message. |
| –1718 | Reply has not yet arrived. |

# Read

The Read command reads data from a file, starting from the file mark and continuing to the end of the file.

Read is one of several commands provided by the Read/Write Commands scripting addition. For more information about using these commands and sample scripts, see "Using Read/Write Commands," which begins on page 70.

SYNTAX

```
read referenceToFile
     [ from startingByte ]                                                ¬
     [ for bytesToRead | to byteToReadTo                                  ¬
        | until delimiterIncluded | before delimiterExcluded ]           ¬
     [ as className [ using delimiter[s] delimiters ] ]
```

PARAMETERS

referenceToFile

A reference of the form file *nameString* or alias *nameString*, or a file reference number previously obtained with the Open for Access command (see "Notes").
*Class:* Reference or integer

*startingByte*    The offset of the byte from which to begin reading. A positive integer indicates the offset from the beginning of the file, and a negative integer indicates the offset from the end of the file.
*Class:* Integer

*bytesToRead*    The number of bytes to read. If the from *startingByte* parameter is included, the Read command reads *bytesToRead* bytes starting at the specified starting point; otherwise, the Read command begins reading at the file mark. If the value of this parameter is negative, an error occurs.
*Class:* Integer

*byteToReadTo*    The offset of the byte to read to. If the from *startingByte* parameter is included, the Read command reads from the specified starting point to *byteToReadTo*; otherwise, the Read command begins reading at the file mark. A positive integer indicates the offset from the beginning of the file, and a negative integer indicates the offset from the end of the file.
*Class:* Integer

*delimiterIncluded*

A delimiter (such as a tab or return character) to read to. The specified delimiter is included in the read (unless it is an end-of-file delimiter, which is not included). If the from *startingByte* parameter is included, the Read command reads from the specified starting point to the specified delimiter; otherwise, the Read command begins reading at the file mark. *Class:* String

*delimiterExcluded*

A delimiter (such as a tab or return character) to which to read. The specified delimiter is not included in the read. If the from *startingByte* parameter is included, the Read command reads from the specified starting point to the specified delimiter; otherwise, the Read command begins reading at the file mark. *Class:* String

*className*

The class of the data to be read. The Read command reads the number of bytes appropriate for a value of the class specified by this parameter. (For details, see "Notes" later in this definition.) *Class:* Class

*delimiters*

If the data being read is text-based, you can use this parameter to specify the delimiters the Read command should use when interpreting the data as values of the class specified by *className*. (For details, see "Notes" later in this definition.) *Class:* String or constant, or a two-item list of strings or constants

**RESULT**

If the Read command is successful, it returns the data read from the file as text (unless specified otherwise by the as parameter).

**EXAMPLES**

This example reads MyFile from the 12th byte and to the end of the file.

```
read file "Hard Disk:MyFile" from 12
```

The next example reads MyFile from the 12th byte before the end of the file to the end of the file.

```
read file "Hard Disk:MyFile" from -12
```

The next example reads 24 bytes of MyFile starting at the 12th byte. If the end of the file is reached before 24 bytes have been read, an error is returned.

```
read file "Hard Disk:MyFile" from 12 for 24
```

The next example reads MyFile starting at the end of the file and reading backward until the third byte from the end.

```
read file "Hard Disk:MyFile" from -1 to -3
```

If the last characters of file MyFile were "123456", the preceding example would return "654".

**NOTES**

The file mark is a marker used by the File Manager that indicates the byte at which the Read command expects to begin reading data. By default, the file mark is the first byte of the file. However, running a script like this causes the file mark for MyFile to be moved:

```
read file "Hard Disk:MyFile" from 1 to 4
```

The file mark for MyFile is now at byte 5, so the next Read command in the same script begins at byte 5. For example, the command

```
read file "Hard Disk:MyFile" for 4
```

reads bytes 5 through 8.

To specify the name (*nameString*) of a file, use a string of the form "*Disk*:*Folder1*:*Folder2*:...:*Filename*" as described in Chapter 5, "Objects and References," of the *AppleScript Language Guide.* If you specify only the name of the file (*Filename*) instead of its entire pathname, AppleScript attempts to find the file in the current directory.

If you specify a reference to a file or an alias, the Read command attempts to match the reference with a file previously opened with the Open for Access command. If a match is found, it simply reads the specified data. If no match is found, the Read command opens the file, reads the specified data, then closes the file. The file mark for a file opened in this fashion is always at the beginning of the file.

If you specify a file reference number previously obtained with the Open for Access command, the Read command reads the specified data immediately.

You can use the `as` *className* parameter to specify how the Read command should interpret the data it reads. If data to be read is not a valid value for the specified value class, the Read command returns an error. The rest of this section describes some of the value classes you can specify and the nature of the data returned if the Read command reads the data successfully.

as list
: The Read command returns a list only if the data to be read was written to disk as an AppleScript list. If the data to be read is delimited text, you can specify the delimiters used in the data with the `using delimiter` parameter, and the Read command creates an AppleScript list based on those delimiters.

  For example, this script returns a list of items from MyFile using both tab and return characters in MyFile to separate each item in the list:

  ```
  read file "Hard Disk:MyFile" as {text} ¬
     using delimiters {return, tab}
  ```

  The resulting list, like any other AppleScript list, is comma-delimited. You can't specify more than two delimiters; if you do, Read returns the error –50.

as record
: Read returns a record only if the data being read was written to disk as an AppleScript record. Read can't coerce other values to records.

as integer
: If the data consists of a single integer, Read returns the integer. If the data consists of more than one integer, Read returns a list of integers.

as text
: Read returns the data as a string. This is the default behavior if the `as` *className* parameter is omitted.

as real
: If the data consists of a single real number, Read returns the real number. If the data consists of more than one real number, Read returns a list of real numbers.

as short
: The short value is defined by the Read/Write Commands scripting addition as 2 bytes long. This can be is useful if you are reading data from a file that uses short integers rather than the 4-byte integers defined by AppleScript. Read interprets the data as one or more discrete 2-byte values. If the data consists of

more than one short value, Read returns a list of shorts. If the data is text, you can specify the delimiters used in the data with the `using delimiter` parameter, and the Read command attempts to coerce each item between delimiters to a short.

as boolean

If the data consists of a 1-byte Boolean value, Read returns the Boolean value. If the data consists of more than one Boolean value, Read returns a list of Boolean values.

as data

Read returns the data as an uninterpreted stream of hexa-decimal bytes.

You can also specify other types by enclosing the appropriate four-character code in quotation marks. Here's an example.

```
read file "Hard Disk:myFile" as "PICT"
--returns data as type 'PICT'
```

**ERRORS**

| Error number | Error message |
|---|---|
| –38 | File <<name>> wasn't open. |
| –39 | End of file error. |
| –50 | Parameter error. |
| –51 | File reference number error. |
| –108 | Out of memory. |
| –1700 | Can't make some data into the expected type. |
| –1701 | Some parameter is missing for <commandName>. |
| –1704 | Some parameter was invalid. |
| –1705 | Operation involving a list item failed. |
| –1715 | Some parameter wasn't understood. |
| –1718 | Reply has not yet arrived. |

# Round

The Round command rounds or truncates a number to an integer. It is one of two commands provided by the Numerics scripting addition.

By default, Round rounds to the nearest number. You may also include an optional parameter to specify rounding up, down, toward zero, or to the nearest number.

**SYNTAX**

round *number* ¬
    [ rounding ( up | down | toward zero | to nearest ) ]

**PARAMETER**

*number*      The number to round.
                 *Class:* Number

See the examples that follow for demonstrations of the possible values of the rounding parameter.

**RESULT**

The result is an integer: the rounded value.

**EXAMPLES**

```
display dialog "round -3.67: " & (round -3.67) & return & ¬
   "round 3.67: " & (round 3.67)

display dialog "round -3.67 up: " &  ¬
   (round -3.67 rounding up) & return & ¬
   "round 3.67 up: " & (round 3.67 rounding up)

display dialog "round -3.67 down: " & ¬
   (round -3.67 rounding down) & return & ¬
   "round 3.67 down: " & (round 3.6 rounding down)
```

```
display dialog "round -3.67 toward zero: " & ¬
    (round -3.67 rounding toward zero) & return & ¬
    "round 3.67 toward zero: " & ¬
    (round 3.67 rounding toward zero)

display dialog "round -3.67 to nearest: " & ¬
    (round -3.67 rounding to nearest) & return & ¬
    "round 3.67 to nearest: " & ¬
    (round 3.67 rounding to nearest)
```

**ERRORS**

| Error number | Error message |
|---|---|
| –50 | Parameter error. |
| –108 | Out of memory. |
| –1700 | Can't make some data into the expected type. |
| –1701 | Some parameter is missing for <commandName>. |
| –1704 | Some parameter was invalid. |
| –1705 | Operation involving a list item failed. |
| –1708 | <reference> doesn't understand the <commandName> message. |
| –1718 | Reply has not yet arrived. |

## Run Script

The Run Script command runs a specified script or script file. It is the only command provided by the Run Script scripting addition.

**SYNTAX**

```
run script referenceOrString                              ¬
    [ with parameters listOfParameters ]                  ¬
    [ in scriptingComponent ]
```

**PARAMETERS**

*referenceOrString*

A reference of the form `file` *nameString* or `alias` *nameString* that specifies a script file, or a string that consists of a valid script.
*Class:* Reference or string

*listOfParameters*

A list of parameters to be passed to the Run handler of the target.
*Class:* List

*scriptingComponent*

The name of the scripting component to use when running the script.
*Class:* String

**RESULT**

Value returned by script that is run.

**EXAMPLES**

This example runs the script `beep 3`, causing the alert sound to sound three times.

```
run script "beep 3"
```

This example ensures that the script `beep 3` is run by the AppleScript scripting component.

```
run script "beep 3" in "AppleScript"
```

This example runs Run handler in the script file called MyScript.

```
run script file "MyVolume:MyDirectory:MyScript"
```

NOTES

To specify the name (*nameString*) of a script file, use a string of the form
"*Disk*:*Folder1*:*Folder2*:...:*Filename*" as described in Chapter 5, "Objects
and References," of the *AppleScript Language Guide*. If you specify only the
name of the file (*Filename*) instead of its entire pathname, AppleScript
attempts to find the file in the current directory.

ERRORS

| Error number | Error message |
| --- | --- |
| –50 | Parameter error. |
| –108 | Out of memory. |
| –192 | Bad name for file. |
| –1700 | Can't make some data into the expected type. |
| –1701 | Some parameter is missing for <commandName>. |
| –1704 | Some parameter was invalid. |
| –1705 | Operation involving a list item failed. |
| –1708 | <reference> doesn't understand the <commandName> message. |
| –1718 | Reply has not yet arrived. |
| –1750 | Scripting component error. |
| –1751 | Invalid script id. |
| –1753 | Script error. |

## Scripting Components

The Scripting Components command returns a list of the names of the scripting
components currently available to the target application. It is the only
command provided by the Scripting Components scripting addition.

SYNTAX

```
scripting components
```

**RESULT**

A list of strings.

**EXAMPLES**

```
scripting components
--result: {"AppleScript"}
```

**NOTES**

A *scripting component* is a software component, such as AppleScript, that supports the Open Scripting Architecture (OSA). The OSA provides a mechanism, based on Apple events, that allows users to control multiple applications by means of scripts written in a variety of scripting languages. Each scripting language corresponds to a single scripting component. A single scripting language may include several dialects.

**ERROR**

| Error number | Error message |
|---|---|
| –108 | Out of memory. |

# Set EOF

The Set EOF sets the end of a specified file. It is one of several commands provided by the Read/Write Commands scripting addition. For more information about these commands, see "Using Read/Write Commands," which begins on page 70.

**SYNTAX**

```
set eof referenceToFile to integer
```

PARAMETERS

*referenceToFile*
> A reference of the form `file` *nameString* or `alias` *nameString*, or a file reference number returned by a previous call to the Open for Access command.
> *Class:* Reference or integer

*integer*
> The number of bytes to which to set the offset of the end of the file.
> *Class:* Integer

RESULT

None

EXAMPLE

```
set eof file "Hard Disk:Status Reports:Weekly Report" to 10
```

NOTES

To specify the name (*nameString*) of a file, use a string of the form "*Disk*:*Folder1*: *Folder2*:....:*Filename*" as described in Chapter 5, "Objects and References," of the *AppleScript Language Guide*. If you specify only the name of the file (*Filename*) instead of its entire pathname, AppleScript attempts to find the file in the current directory.

If you specify a reference to a file or an alias, the Set EOF command attempts to match the reference with a file previously opened (with write permission) with the Open for Access command. If the file was previously opened with read permission only, Set EOF returns the error code –61. If a match is found, Set EOF sets the end of the file as specified. If no match is found, Set EOF opens the file, sets the end of the file, then closes the file.

If you specify a file reference number previously obtained (with write permission) with the Open for Access command, Set EOF sets the end of the file immediately.

**IMPORTANT**

If the file is longer than the end of file set by Set EOF, it is truncated to the specified size and any additional data is lost. If the file is shorter than the end of file set by Set EOF, it is extended to the new length, but the additional data in the new part of the file is meaningless. ▲

ERRORS

| Error number | Error message |
|---|---|
| –34 | Disk <name> is full. |
| –38 | File <name> wasn't open. |
| –44 | Disk <name> is write protected. |
| –45 | File <name> is locked. |
| –46 | Disk <name> is locked. |
| –50 | Parameter error. |
| –51 | File reference number error. |
| –61 | File not open with write permission. |

# Start Log

The Start Log command turns on logging in the Script Editor's Event Log window, which is shown in Figure 2-7.

If the checkboxes Show Events and Show Event Results are both selected, as shown in Figure 2-7, subsequent commands sent by the Script Editor and the results returned for each event are displayed in this window. You can choose to display either the events or their results by selecting just one of the checkboxes. You can also save a copy of the text in the Event Log window by choosing Save As from the File menu.

Unlike most other scripting additions, the Start Log command is built into the AppleScript extension. It doesn't have a separate file in the Scripting Additions folder.

**Figure 2-7**    The Script Editor's Event Log window

SYNTAX

```
start log
```

RESULT

None

EXAMPLE

The example that follows demonstrates how to start logging and demonstrates how logging works. To see descriptions in AppleScript of the logged events generated by this example, open the Event Log window in the Script Editor application by choosing Open Event Log from the Controls menu. Make sure that both the Show Events and Show Event Results checkboxes are selected, as shown in Figure 2-7.

```
start log
display dialog "Hello"
```

After you run the preceding script, the record of the events sent and the result returned appear in the Event Log window. Because the Display Dialog command in this script is not enclosed in a Tell statement, Script Editor sends the command to the current application—that is, to itself. The event log for the script shows both this implicit Tell statement and the result returned by the Display Dialog command.

**ERRORS**

| Error number | Error message |
|---|---|
| –50 | Parameter error. |
| –108 | Out of memory. |
| –1700 | Can't make some data into the expected type. |
| –1701 | Some parameter is missing for <commandName>. |
| –1704 | Some parameter was invalid. |
| –1705 | Operation involving a list item failed. |
| –1708 | <reference> doesn't understand the <commandName> message. |
| –1718 | Reply has not yet arrived. |

# Stop Log

The Stop Log command turns off logging in the Script Editor's Event Log window. Unlike most other scripting additions, the Stop Log command is built into the AppleScript extension. It does not have a separate file in the Scripting Additions folder.

For more information about the Event Log window, see page 61.

**SYNTAX**

```
stop log
```

**RESULT**

None

**EXAMPLE**

```
stop log
```

**NOTES**

The Log command works even if logging has been turned off with the Stop Log command. If the Stop Log command is sent before the Log command, logging will still be turned off after the Log command is sent.

**ERRORS**

| Error number | Error message |
|---|---|
| –50 | Parameter error. |
| –108 | Out of memory. |
| –1700 | Can't make some data into the expected type. |
| –1701 | Some parameter is missing for <commandName>. |
| –1704 | Some parameter was invalid. |
| –1705 | Operation involving a list item failed. |
| –1708 | <reference> doesn't understand the <commandName> message. |
| –1718 | Reply has not yet arrived. |

# Store Script

The Store Script command stores a specified script object in a specified file. It is the only command provided by the Store Script scripting addition.

**SYNTAX**

```
store script scriptObjectVariable                    ¬
    [in referenceToFile ]                            ¬
    [ replacing replacementOption ]
```

**PARAMETERS**

*scriptObjectVariable*

The name of a script object declared previously in the same script.
*Class:* Script

*referenceToFile*

A reference of the form `file` *nameString* or `alias` *nameString* (see "Notes"). If this parameter is omitted, Store Script displays a directory dialog box and requests that the user choose a file in which to store the script.
*Class:* Reference

*replacementOption*

One of the constants `ask`, `yes`, or `no`. The constant `ask` causes the Store Script command to display a dialog box asking the user whether to overwrite the file specified by *scriptObjectVariable*, rename it, or cancel the operation. (Displaying this dialog box is the default if the `replacing` parameter is omitted.) The constant `yes` indicates that you want Store Script to replace the file, and the constant `no` indicates that you do not want Store Script to replace the file if it already exists.
*Class:* String

**RESULT**

None

**EXAMPLES**

This script object is used in the examples that follow:

```
script DemoStore
    property Red: 127
    property Green : 128
    property Blue : 127
    on returnRGB()
        return Red & Green & Blue
    end return
end script
```

This example stores the script object `DemoStore` in a file called Store My RGB:

```
store script DemoStore in file ¬
    "My HD:Some Folder:Store My RGB" replacing yes
```

The `replacing yes` parameter indicates that Store Script should overwrite the existing file.

Later statements in the same script like the following load the stored script object `DemoStore`, change one of its properties, and store it to disk again:

```
set objRef to load script ¬
    file "My HD:Some Folder:Store My RGB"
set objRef's Red to 250
store script objRef ¬
    in file "My HD:Some Folder:Store My RGB"
```

In this case the `replacing` parameter is omitted, so Store Script displays a dialog box asking the user whether to overwrite the file, rename it, or cancel the operation.

**NOTES**

To specify the name (*nameString*) of a file, use a string of the form "*Disk*: *Folder1*: *Folder2*: . . . : *Filename*" as described in Chapter 5, "Objects and References," of the *AppleScript Language Guide*. If you specify only the name of the file (*Filename*) instead of its entire pathname, AppleScript attempts to find the file in the current directory.

**ERRORS**

| Error number | Error message |
| --- | --- |
| –108 | Out of memory. |
| –128 | User canceled. |
| –192 | Bad name for file. |
| –1700 | Can't make some data into the expected type. |
| –1701 | Some parameter is missing for <commandName>. |

| Error number | Error message |
|---|---|
| –1704 | Some parameter was invalid. |
| –1705 | Operation involving a list item failed. |
| –1708 | <reference> doesn't understand the <commandName> message. |
| –1718 | Reply has not yet arrived. |

# Time to GMT

The Time to GMT command returns the difference, in seconds, between the current time and Greenwich mean time (GMT). It is the only command provided by the Time to GMT scripting addition.

### SYNTAX

```
time to GMT
```

### PARAMETERS

None.

### RESULT

An integer indicating the difference in seconds between the current time and GMT.

### EXAMPLES

Time to GMT returns the difference in seconds between the time of your computer's clock and GMT. For example, if you are in Cupertino, California, and your computer is set to Pacific Standard Time, Time to GMT returns this result:

```
time to GMT
--result: -28800
```

You can then use this value to write a script that tells you the time difference between the time in any other time zone and the current time in Cupertino:

```
property offsetFromCupertino : -28800

set x to ((time to GMT) ÷ 60) ÷ 60
set y to x - (((offsetFromCupertino) ÷ 60) ÷ 60)

if y = 0 then
    display dialog ("Same time zone as Cupertino") as string
else
    if y > 0 then
        display dialog (y & " Hours Ahead of Cupertino") as
string
    else
        display dialog (-y & " Hours Behind Cupertino") as
string
    end if
end if
```

To see the effect this script has for different time zones, try setting the time from the Map control panel to various locations, for example, Tokyo, London, and Atlanta.

**ERRORS**

| Error number | Error message |
| --- | --- |
| –108 | Out of memory. |
| –1700 | Can't make some data into the expected type. |
| –1701 | Some parameter is missing for <commandName>. |
| –1704 | Some parameter was invalid. |
| –1705 | Operation involving a list item failed. |
| –1708 | <reference> doesn't understand the <commandName> message. |
| –1718 | Reply has not yet arrived. |

# Write

The Write command writes data to a specified file, beginning at the file mark. It is one of several commands provided by the Read/Write Commands scripting addition. For more information about these commands, see "Using Read/Write Commands," which begins on page 70.

**SYNTAX**

```
write dataToWrite to referenceToFile
    [ for bytesToWrite ] ¬
    [ starting at startingByte ]
```

**PARAMETERS**

*dataToWrite*    The data to be written. The format of the data should match the file type.
*Class:* (varies among applications)

*referenceToFile*
A reference of the form `file` *nameString* or `alias` *nameString*, or a file reference number previously obtained with the Open for Access command (see "Notes").
*Class:* Reference or integer

*bytesToWrite*    The number of bytes to write. The Write command returns an error if you pass a negative number in this parameter.
*Class:* Integer

*startingByte*    Specifies the offset of the byte at which to begin writing. A positive integer indicates the offset from the beginning of the file, and a negative integer indicates the offset from the end of the file.
*Class:* Integer

**RESULT**

None

**EXAMPLES**

This example writes "abcde" to the file MyFile.

```
write "abcde" to file "Hard Disk:MyFile"
```

The next example returns an error because fewer bytes are specified for the *dataToWrite* parameter than are specified for the `for` *bytesToWrite* parameter:

```
write "abcde" to file "Hard Disk:MyFile" for 8
```

If the data to write is longer than the bytes specified by the *bytesToWrite* parameter, the Write command truncates the data. For example, this Write command writes the number 5 to the file MyFile as a short integer (2 bytes) rather than an integer (4 bytes):

```
write 5 to file "Hard Disk:MyFile" for 2
```

The next example specifies a negative value for the *startingByte* parameter. It writes the number 5 as a short integer starting at the 8th byte before the end of the file.

```
write 5 to file "Hard Disk:MyFile" starting at -8 for 2
```

**NOTES**

The file mark is a marker used by the File Manager that indicates the byte at which the Read command expects to begin reading data. By default, the file mark is the first byte of the file. The Write command begins writing at the current file mark and sets the file mark to the byte after the last byte written. The Read command can also reset the file mark.

To set the file mark without reading or writing data, write a string of zero length to the byte to which you want to set the mark. For example, this script sets the file mark for the file specified by `fileRefNum` to the fourth byte in the file:

```
write "" to fileRefNum starting at 4
```

To specify the name (*nameString*) of a file, use a string of the form "*Disk*:*Folder1*: *Folder2*:...:*Filename*" as described in Chapter 5, "Objects and References," of the *AppleScript Language Guide*. If you specify only the name of the file (*Filename*) instead of its entire pathname, AppleScript attempts to find the file in the current directory

The Write command attempts to match a reference to a file or an alias with a file previously opened with the Open for Access command. If a match is found, it simply writes the specified data. If no match is found but the file can be located on disk, the Write command opens the file, writes the specified data, then closes the file. The file mark for a file opened in this fashion is always at the beginning of the file. If the file cannot be found at all, the Write command returns an error.

If you specify a file reference number previously obtained with the Open for Access command, the Write command writes the specified data immediately.

ERRORS

| Error number | Error message |
|---|---|
| –34 | Disk <name> is full. |
| –38 | File <name> wasn't open. |
| –44 | Disk <name> is write protected. |
| –45 | File <name> is locked. |
| –49 | File <name> is already open. |
| –50 | Parameter error. |
| –51 | File reference number error. |
| –61 | File not open with write permission. |
| –108 | Out of memory. |

# Using Read/Write Commands

The commands provided by the Read/Write Commands scripting addition allow you to open a file for access, get and set its length, read data from the file, insert new data in the file, and close access to the file. These commands allow you to make use, from within a script, of some capabilities of the File Manager, the part of the Macintosh Operating System that controls files.

▲ **WARNING**
The Read/Write Commands scripting addition is intended for use by experienced programmers. If you are not familiar with the File Manager as described in *Inside Macintosh: Files*, proceed with caution. Using these commands incorrectly may cause loss of data. ▲

Most of the Read/Write Commands allow you to specify a file reference number instead of a reference to a file. A file reference number is an integer, assigned by the File Manager, that uniquely identifies a file. You can obtain a file reference number with the Open for Access command, then use the number returned to refer to the same file until you use the Close Access command to close the file. It is usually preferable to specify a file reference number rather than a reference to a file because it takes the Read/Write Commands scripting addition less time to locate the file.

You can use the Read/Write commands with either text-based data or binary data. Most databases can export data as text, with fields and records separated by delimiters, and some store their data as text files. The examples in this section demonstrate how to use the Read/Write commands with text-based data. These examples assume that you have basic information about the way the data is stored in a text file, such as the delimiters used to separate fields and records. You can use similar techniques to read and write binary data if you know how the data is organized within a file. For example, if you know the header format for a file of type 'PICT', you can write scripts that read and write to 'PICT' files.

Both the Read command and the Write command make use of the *file mark*, a marker used by the File Manager that indicates the byte at which the Read and Write commands begin operating. By default, the file mark is the first byte of the file. After the Read command reads a range of bytes or the Write command writes over a range of bytes, the file mark is set to byte just after the end of that range. The next Read or Write command begins operating at the new file mark.

For example, suppose you want to extract a particular record from a text-based database of names and addresses. To do so, you need to know the number of fields in each record, the position of the desired record in the database, and the delimiters used to separate the records in the database. You can then use the Open for Access command to get a file reference number for the file that contains the desired record and a Read command within a repeat loop to read each successive record. After reading each record, the Read command sets the file mark to the beginning of the next record. When the repeat loop determines that the desired record has been reached, it returns the data for that record. Listing 2-1 shows one way to do this.

**Listing 2-1**     Reading a specific record from a text-based database file

```
--first choose data file to work with
set pathToUse to choose file

try
    set x to open for access pathToUse
    set z to ReadRecord(10, 1, tab, return, x)
    close access x
    z --display requested record
on error errString number errNum
    display dialog errString
    close access x
end try


on ReadRecord(numberOfFields, whichRecord, fieldDelimiter, ¬
            recordDelimiter, fileRefNum)
    try
        (* if there's a record delimiter, read all fields except for
        last using field delimiter, then read last field using record
        delimiter *)
        if recordDelimiter is "" then
            set readxTimes to numberOfFields
        else
            set readxTimes to numberOfFields - 1
        end if
        repeat whichRecord times
            set recordData to {}
            repeat (readxTimes) times
                set recordData to recordData & ¬
                    {(read fileRefNum before fieldDelimiter)}
            end repeat
            if readxTimes is not numberOfFields then
                set recordData to recordData & ¬
                    {(read fileRefNum before recordDelimiter)}
            end if
        end repeat
        return recordData
```

```
    on error errString number errNum
        display dialog errString
        return errString
    end try
end ReadRecord
```

The script in Listing 2-1 begins by using the Choose File command to allow the user to choose the text file that contains the desired record. After initializing the variable into which the record will be read, the script uses the Open for Access command to open the file and the ReadRecord handler to read a specific record.

The ReadRecord handler shown in Listing 2-1 takes five parameters:

numberOfFields
> The number of fields in the record.

whichRecord
> An integer that identifies the position of the desired record.

fieldDelimiter
> The delimiter used in the file to separate fields.

recordDelimiter
> The delimiter (if any) used to separate records. If the file doesn't use a different delimiter to separate records, this parameter must be set to " ".

fileRefNum A file reference number obtained with the Open for Access command.

If recordDelimiter is set to " ", the ReadRecord handler reads the specified number of fields for each record. If recordDelimiter is set to a delimiter, ReadRecord reads all the fields in a record but the last, then reads the last field up to the record delimiter. This is necessary to ensure that the last field of one record is not combined with the first field of the next.

The ReadRecord handler reads each new record into the variable recordData. If the record is the one requested, ReadRecord returns that record. If the record is not the requested record, ReadRecord sets recordData to an empty list and reads the next record.

You can use similar techniques to locate the exact position of a record you want to delete from a text file. In addition to locating the record to be deleted, you need to store all the records after that record in a variable and write the contents of the variable starting at the beginning of the record to be deleted.

You can then use the Get EOF and Set EOF commands to get the initial size of
the file and reset its size after deleting the record. Listing 2-2 demonstrates how
to do this.

**Listing 2-2**      Deleting a record from a text-based database file

```
--choose data file to use
set pathToUse to choose file

try
    set x to open for access pathToUse with write permission
    DeleteRecord(10, 1, tab, return, x)
    close access x
on error errString number errNum
    display dialog errString
    close access x
end try

on DeleteRecord(numberOfFields, whichRecord, ¬
            fieldDelimiter, recordDelimiter, fileRefNum)
    try
        --initialize variables
        set startSize to get eof fileRefNum --current size
        set idx to 1 --counter
        set preRecordSize to 1 --offset of record to delete
        set accumulatedSize to 0 --total size of records read

        if recordDelimiter is "" then
            set readxTimes to numberOfFields
        else
            set readxTimes to numberOfFields - 1
        end if
```

```
repeat with idx from 1 to whichRecord
    repeat (readxTimes) times
        set q to read fileRefNum until fieldDelimiter
        set accumulatedSize to accumulatedSize + (length of q)
    end repeat

    if readxTimes is not numberOfFields then
        set q to read fileRefNum until recordDelimiter
        set accumulatedSize to accumulatedSize + (length of q)
    end if

    (* if record to delete is the first record in file or the
    next record that will be read, set preRecordSize *)
    if whichRecord is 1 or idx is whichRecord - 1 then
        if whichRecord is 1 then
            set preRecordSize to 1
        else
            set preRecordSize to accumulatedSize
        end if
    end if
end repeat

(* now that preRecordSize is determined, read the record to be
deleted so file mark is set to beginning of next record *)
set fileBuffer to read fileRefNum from accumulatedSize + 1

--next, overwrite record to be deleted with remainder of file
if (startSize - accumulatedSize) is not 0 then
    write fileBuffer to fileRefNum starting at preRecordSize
    set eof fileRefNum to (startSize - accumulatedSize)
else
    (* if the file contains only the record to be
    deleted, set the end of the file to 0 *)
    if whichRecord is 1 then
        set eof fileRefNum to 0
```

```
        (* if record to be deleted is last record in file,
        just shrink the file *)
        else
            set eof fileRefNum to preRecordSize
        end if
    end if
on error errString number errNum
    display dialog errString
end try
end DeleteRecord
```

The `DeleteRecord` handler shown in Listing 2-2 takes five parameters:

`numberOfFields`

> The number of fields in each record.

`whichRecord`

> An integer that identifies the position of the record you want to delete.

`fieldDelimiter`

> The delimiter used in the file to separate fields.

`recordDelimiter`

> The delimiter (if any) used to separate records. If the file doesn't use a different delimiter to separate records, this parameter must be set to `" "`.

`fileRefNum`

> A file reference number obtained with the Open for Access command.

Like the `ReadRecord` handler in Listing 2-1, the `DeleteRecord` handler reads the specified number of fields for each record if `recordDelimiter` is set to `" "`. If `recordDelimiter` is set to a delimiter, `DeleteRecord` reads all the fields in a record but the last, then reads the last field up to the record delimiter. The size of each successive record is added to the `accumulatedSize` variable, which contains the total size of the previously read records.

When it reaches the record to be deleted, `DeleteRecord` stores the contents of `accumulatedSize` in the `preRecordSize` variable, reads through the record to set the file mark, reads from the file mark to the end of the file, and stores that portion of the file in the `fileBuffer` variable. Finally, `DeleteRecord` writes the contents of `fileBuffer` starting at the beginning of the record to be deleted.

Listing 2-3 demonstrates how you can use similar techniques to insert a record into a text-based database file.

**Listing 2-3**     Inserting a record in a database file

```
--choose file to work with
set pathToUse to choose file

try
    (* first put the record to be added into a variable; in this case
    the record to be added is actually an AppleScript list because
    the file on disk doesn't include label data *)
    set newRecord to ¬
        {"Granny", "Smith", "123  Potato Chip Lane", ¬
        "Palo Minnow", "CA", "98761", "Snackable Computer", ¬
        "888-987-0987", "978 -234-5432", "123-985-1122"}
    set x to open for access pathToUse with write permission
    AddRecord(newRecord, 5, tab, return, x)
    close access x

on error errString number errNum
    display dialog errString
    close access x
end try

on AddRecord(recordToAdd, addWhere, fieldDelimiter, ¬
            recordDelimiter, fileRefNum)
    try
        --initialize variables
        set idx to 1 --counter
        set preRecordSize to 1 --offset of byte at which to add file
        set accumulatedSize to 0 --total size of records read
        set numberOfFields to count of recordToAdd
```

```
if recordDelimiter is "" then
    set readxTimes to numberOfFields
else
    set readxTimes to numberOfFields - 1
end if

(* if the record is to be added at the beginning of the file,
this If statement adds the record *)
if addWhere is 1 then
    --read from beginning of file and store in postBuffer
    set postBuffer to read fileRefNum from 1
    (* before writing new record, file mark must be reset to
    beginning of file; to do this, write an empty string to the
    beginning of file *)
    write "" to fileRefNum starting at 0
    WriteNewRecord(recordToAdd, fieldDelimiter, ¬
                   recordDelimiter, fileRefNum)
    --now add back the rest of the record
    write postBuffer to fileRefNum
    return
end if
(* if the record is to be added somewhere other than at the
beginning of the file, the rest of the AddRecord handler is
executed *)

repeat with idx from 1 to addWhere - 1
    repeat (readxTimes) times
        set q to read fileRefNum until fieldDelimiter
        set accumulatedSize to accumulatedSize + (length of q)
    end repeat
    if readxTimes is not numberOfFields then
        set q to read fileRefNum until recordDelimiter
        set accumulatedSize to accumulatedSize + (length of q)
    end if
end repeat
```

```
(* read from beginning of file to the byte at which the new
record is to be added *)
set postBuffer to read fileRefNum from accumulatedSize + 1

(* before writing new record, set file mark to byte at which
new record is to be added; to do this, write an empty
string to that byte *)
write "" to fileRefNum starting at accumulatedSize + 1
WriteNewRecord(recordToAdd, fieldDelimiter, recordDelimiter, ¬
            fileRefNum)
--now add back the rest of the record
write postBuffer to fileRefNum

    on error errString number errNum
        display dialog errString
    end try
end AddRecord


on WriteNewRecord(recordToAdd, fieldDelimiter, recordDelimiter,¬
            fileRefNum)
    try
        set numberOfFields to count of recordToAdd
        if recordDelimiter is "" then
            set readxTimes to numberOfFields
        else
            set readxTimes to numberOfFields - 1
        end if

        repeat with idx from 1 to numberOfFields
            if idx ≤ readxTimes then
                write item idx of recordToAdd & fieldDelimiter to ¬
                    fileRefNum
```

```
        else
            (* if file uses a record delimiter, write delimiter
            after the last field in the record *)
            write item idx of recordToAdd & recordDelimiter to ¬
                fileRefNum
        end if
    end repeat
on error errString number errNum
    display dialog errString
end try
end WriteNewRecord
```

The `AddRecord` handler shown in Listing 2-3 takes five parameters:

`recordToAdd`

> A list of the fields for the record to be added.

`whichRecord`

> An integer that identifies the offset of the record you want to add.

`fieldDelimiter`

> The delimiter used in the file to separate fields.

`recordDelimiter`

> The delimiter (if any) used to separate records. If the file doesn't use a different delimiter to separate records, this parameter must be set to `" "`.

`fileRefNum`

> A file reference number obtained with the Open for Access command.

If the new record is to be added at the beginning of the file, AddRecord reads all the records in the file and stores them in the `postBuffer` variable, then resets the file mark to the beginning of the file by writing an empty string to that location. This is a useful technique whenever you want to set the file mark without reading or writing any data.

Next, `AddRecord` uses the `WriteNewRecord` handler to write the record at the beginning of the file and writes the contents of the `postBuffer` variable after the new record. Note that the Write Command sets the end of file, so this example doesn't need to use the Get EOF and Set EOF commands.

If the new record is to be added somewhere other than at the beginning of the file, `AddRecord` uses a repeat loop to read through all the records that precede the new record's location. If `recordDelimiter` is set to `""`, `AddRecord` reads the specified number of fields for each record. If `recordDelimiter` is set to a delimiter, `AddRecord` reads all the fields in a record but the last, then reads the last field up to the record delimiter. The size of each successive record is added to the `accumulatedSize` variable, which contains the total size of the previously read records.

After it has stored, in the `accumulatedSize` variable, the total size of the records preceding the point at which the new record is to be added, `AddRecord` reads the remainder of the file and stores it in the `postBuffer` variable. It then resets the file mark to the byte at which the new record is to be added by writing an empty string to that location. After using the `WriteNewRecord` handler to write the record, `AddRecord` writes the contents of the `postBuffer` variable after the new record.

The `WriteNewRecord` handler shown in Listing 2-3 takes four parameters:

`recordToAdd`
> A list of the fields for the record to be added.

`fieldDelimiter`
> The delimiter used in the file to separate fields.

`recordDelimiter`
> The delimiter (if any) used to separate records. If the file doesn't use a different delimiter to separate records, this parameter must be set to `""`.

`fileRefNum` A file reference number obtained with the Open for Access command.

If `recordDelimiter` is set to `""`, `WriteNewRecord` includes a field delimiter after each field it writes. If `recordDelimiter` is set to a delimiter, `WriteNewRecord` includes a field delimiter after each field in a record but the last and includes a record delimiter after the last field.

Listing 2-4 demonstrates one way to take advantage of the fact that the Open for Access command can create a file with a specified name in a specified location if the file doesn't already exist at that location.

**Listing 2-4**     Opening a file for write access and creating one if the file doesn't exist

```
on OpenFileIfItExists(theFile, writePermission)
   try
      (* if theFile doesn't exist, Info For returns error -43 *)
      set x to info for file theFile
      if writePermission is true then
         return (open for access file theFile with write permission)
      else
         return (open for access file theFile)
      end if
   on error theErrMsg number errorNum
      try
         --if error is -43, the user can choose to create the file
         display dialog "The file: " & theFile & " does not exist" ¬
            buttons {"Create It For Me", "Cancel", "Ok"} ¬
            default button 2
         if button returned of the result is "Ok" then
            return errorNum

         else
            --create the file
            if writePermission is true then
               return open for access file theFile ¬
                  with write permission
            else
               return open for access file theFile
            end if
         end if
      on error theErrMsg number theErrNumber
         return theErrNumber
      end try
   end try
end OpenFileIfItExists
```

```
--set a variable to the file you want to open or create
set fileToOpenOrCreate to "Hard Disk:Test File One"

set z to OpenFileIfItExists(fileToOpenOrCreate, true)
if z < 0 then
   --OpenFileIfItExists returned an error
   display dialog the result

else
   --OpenFileIfItExists returned a file reference number
   --do your work with the open file here
   close access z
end if
```

The `OpenFileIfItExists` handler shown in Listing 2-4 takes two parameters:

`theFile`       A string that consists of the full pathname for the file to open or create.

`writePermission`
A Boolean value that indicates whether to open the file with (`true`) or without (`false`) write permission.

To determine whether the file exists or not, `OpenFileIfItExists` uses the Info For command. If the file doesn't exist, the Info For command returns error –43, "File wasn't found," and `OpenFileIfItExists` displays a dialog box that allows the user to choose whether to create the new file. If the file exists or if it is successfully created, `OpenFileIfItExists` opens it with or without write permission, depending on the value of the `writePermission` parameter.

# Writing Scripting Additions

This chapter is intended for experienced Macintosh programmers. Before reading this chapter, you should have a thorough understanding of the Apple Event Manager, Apple event terminology resources, and the C or Pascal programming language. For information about the Apple Event Manager and Apple event terminology resources, see *Inside Macintosh: Interapplication Communication*.

This chapter describes

- types of scripting additions
- the scripting addition size resource
- how to use other resources with scripting additions
- a trick for using records as scripting addition reply values
- scripting addition limitations

It also includes code written in C for a sample scripting addition.

## Types of Scripting Additions

There are two types of scripting additions:

- Apple event handler scripting additions (language extensions)
- Apple event coercion scripting additions (data coercions)

Both types are loaded by the AppleScript extension when needed if the scripting addition files are installed in the Scripting Additions folder. Each type of scripting addition consists of a file of type `'osax'` and a creator of type `'ascr'`. The name of the `'osax'` resource tells the scripting addition loading mechanism what type of scripting addition it is.

A scripting addition resource file may contain up to four kinds of resource:
(1) a code resource of type 'osax' that contains the executable code for the
scripting addition, (2) an 'aete' resource that describes the terminology
provided by the scripting addition, (3) a resource of type 'osiz' that informs
AppleScript whether the scripting addition has any owned resources and
whether it responds to commands sent from other computers on a network,
and (4) any owned resources for the scripting addition, such as dialog
definitions, strings, and sounds.

The next two sections describe the differences between 'osax' resources
for Apple event handlers and 'osax' resources for Apple event coercions.
For information about writing an 'aete' resource, see *Inside Macintosh:
Interapplication Communication.* "The Scripting Addition Size Resource," which
begins on page 89, describes the format of the 'osiz' resource.

## Apple Event Handler Scripting Addition

The 'osax' resource for an Apple event handler follows the following
convention:

Resource type       'osax'

Resource ID         An identifier (for example, 6991)

Resource name       'AEVTclssidid'

The letters AEVT in the resource name indicate that the scripting addition uses
the event handler interface. The next eight characters represent the event's class
and ID.

The 'osax' code resource for a scripting addition handler is in the form of
an Apple event handler. The entry point for the code resource must follow the
Apple event handler function interface as follows:

In C,

```
pascal OSErr MyAEHandlerFunction (AppleEvent theEvent,
                                  AppleEvent theReply,
                                  long theRefCon);
```

In Pascal,

```
FUNCTION MyAEHandlerFunction
                    (theEvent, theReply: AppleEvent;
                     theRefCon: Longint): OSErr;
```

The scripting addition handler is an extension to the AppleScript language. It needs an 'aete' resource that describes the human-language terms defined by the scripting addition for use in scripts, such as the names of commands, objects, and properties. The high word of the resource ID for the 'aete' is a script code that indicates the script system (that is, writing system) for which the 'aete' is written, and the low word is a language code that indicates the human language for which the 'aete' is written. For example, the resource ID of the 'aete' resource of the sample scripting addition shown in Listing 3-3 (beginning on page 94) is 0; thus both the high word and low word are also 0, indicating that the resource is intended for use with the Roman script system and English terminology.

## Apple Event Coercions Scripting Addition

The 'osax' resource for an Apple event coercion scripting addition follows the following convention:

| | |
|---|---|
| Resource type | 'osax' |
| Resource ID | An identifier (for example, 3069) |
| Resource name | 'CSDSfromtoto' or 'CSPTfromtoto' |

The letters CSDS or CSPT at the beginning of the resource name indicate that the scripting addition provides an Apple event coercion. CSDS indicates an Apple event coercion that uses the "from descriptor" interface. CSPT indicates an Apple event coercion that uses the "coerce from pointer" interface. The next eight characters of the resource name represent the "from" and "to" types.

The 'osax' code resource for scripting addition coercions is in the form of Apple event coercion handler. The entry point for the code resource must follow the Apple event coercion function interface for the particular coercion form.

In C, the "coerce from pointer" coercion form (CSPT) is

```
pascal OSErr MyCoercePtr (DescType fromType,
                          Ptr dataPtr,
                          Size dataSize,
                          DescType toType,
                          long theRefCon,
                          AEDesc *theResult);
```

In Pascal, the "coerce from pointer" coercion form (CSPT) is

```
FUNCTION MyCoercePtr (typeCode:DescType;
                      dataPtr: Ptr;
                      dataSize: Size;
                      toType: DescType;
                      refcon: LongInt;
                      VAR addressDesc: AEDesc): OSErr;
```

In C, the "coerce from descriptor" coercion form (CSDS) is

```
pascal OSErr MyCoerceDesc (AEDesc theFromDesc,
                           DescType toType,
                           long theRefCon,
                           AEDesc *theResult);
```

In Pascal, the "coerce from descriptor" coercion form (CSDS) is

```
FUNCTION MyCoerceDesc (theFromDesc: AEDesc;
                       toType: DescType;
                       theRefCon: LongInt;
                       VAR addressDesc: AEDesc): OSErr;
```

# The Scripting Addition Size Resource

If your scripting addition doesn't include any owned resources, you can improve its performance by providing a scripting addition size resource. A scripting addition size resource is a resource of type 'osiz' that allows you to specify whether your scripting addition has any owned resources and whether to limit the events it can receive to events sent from the local computer.

An 'osiz' resource must have resource ID 0. Listing 3-1 shows the resource type declaration in Rez format for the 'osiz' resource.

**Listing 3-1** Resource type declaration for the 'osiz' resource

```
type 'osiz' {
        boolean   openResourceFile,
                  dontOpenResourceFile;
        boolean   acceptRemoteEvents,
                  dontAcceptRemoteEvents;
        boolean   reserved;
        boolean   reserved;
        boolean   reserved;
        boolean   reserved;
        boolean   reserved;
        boolean   reserved;
        boolean   reserved;
        boolean   reserved;
        boolean   reserved;
        boolean   reserved;
        boolean   reserved;
        boolean   reserved;
        boolean   reserved;
        boolean   reserved;
        boolean   reserved;
```

```
    boolean    reserved;
    boolean    reserved;
    boolean    reserved;
    boolean    reserved;
    boolean    reserved;
    boolean    reserved;
    boolean    reserved;
    boolean    reserved;
    boolean    reserved;
    boolean    reserved;
    boolean    reserved;
    boolean    reserved;
    boolean    reserved;
    boolean    reserved;
    boolean    reserved;
};
```

The data for an `'osiz'` resource consists of flags that specify Boolean values:

■ The first flag specifies whether AppleScript should (`openResourceFile`)
   or should not (`dontOpenResourceFile`) open the scripting addition's
   resource fork each time one of its commands is invoked from a script. You
   should set this flag to `dontOpenResourceFile` if your scripting addition
   doesn't include any owned resources.

■ The second flag specifies whether the scripting addition accepts
   (`acceptRemoteEvents`) or doesn't accept (`dontAcceptRemoteEvents`)
   events sent to it from a remote computer. If you don't want users of remote
   computers to be able to use your scripting addition, set this flag to
   `dontAcceptRemoteEvents`. This might be desirable, for example, if you
   don't want users of remote computers to use the scripting addition to
   modify data on the local machine or if the scripting addition requires
   interaction with the user.

■ The following 30 bits are reserved for future use. Their values must be set to
   `reserved`.

# Using Other Resources With Scripting Additions

The scripting addition loading mechanism adds the invoked scripting addition's resource file to the top of the target application's resource chain. This guarantees that resources in the scripting addition's resource file will be found before resources with the same name or ID in the application or system resource files. For example, in the following script, the resource chain is: Beep scripting addition -> MyApplication -> System file (assuming MyApplication hasn't added anything else to the chain).

```
tell application "MyApplication"
    beep 3
end tell
```

If a scripting addition is called outside of a Tell statement, the resource chain is the same as just described, except that the application is the application running the script (for example, Script Editor).

# Using Records for Scripting Addition Reply Values

Some scripting additions return more than one piece of data in their replies. If a scripting addition returns a list, it can refer to the elements of the list by index. But if a scripting addition returns a record with named fields, it cannot refer to the items in the record by their names, because although an 'aete' resource allows you to specify the type of a return value, it does not provide any additional information about it, such as the names of its fields if it is a record.

If you need that additional information, you can create a new class that has properties for each of the fields in the record, and you can then declare the return type of the reply to be the ID of this new class.

Listing 3-2 shows an 'aete' code excerpt that defines a class with the ID 'hack'. This code is placed in the return type field of the event's reply. The property IDs are the keywords for the record's fields.

Listing 3-2     Classes array for a scripting addition that returns a record

```
{   /* array Classes: 1 elements */
    /* [1] */
    "my record names",
    'hack',
    "A demo class used for record labels",
    {   /* array Properties: 2 elements */
        /* [1] */
        "button returned",
        'rone',
        ' hack',
        "The button returned",
        reserved,
        singleItem,
        notEnumerated,
        readOnly,
        reserved, reserved, reserved, reserved, reserved, reserved,
        reserved, reserved, reserved, reserved, reserved, reserved,
        /* [2] */
        "text returned",
        'rtwo',
        'hack',
        "The text returned",
        reserved,
        singleItem,
        notEnumerated,
        readOnly,
        reserved, reserved, reserved, reserved, reserved, reserved,
        reserved, reserved, reserved, reserved, reserved, reserved
    },
},
```

For an example of this technique in action, see the reply returned by the Display Dialog scripting addition.

# Scripting Addition Limitations

Scripting additions are stand-alone code resources. As such they cannot have global variables. Solutions are available to circumvent this limitation in code resources. Check your compiler documentation for these solutions or see the appropriate technical notes from Apple Computer.

Scripting additions cannot use the Object Support Library (OSL). The OSL is designed to be linked into an application and initialized once. This means that a scripting addition that has to resolve object specifier records must do so internally without the use of the OSL.

Scripting additions are not chained. If two or more scripting additions in the Scripting Additions folder have the same class and ID, only the first one found (that is, the first one in alphabetical order by name) will be installed.

# Sample Scripting Addition

Listing 3-3 demonstrates the basic structure of a scripting addition handler and its associated 'aete' resource. It is called "Play Sound Scripting Addition" and is written in MPW C.

**Listing 3-3**     Play Sound scripting addition

```
///////////////////////////////////////////////////////////////
//
// PlaySnd.c
//
// The Play Sound Scripting Addition
// Copyright ®1993 Apple Computer Inc.
// All rights reserved.
//
// Written by: Donald Olson
//
// To build:
// C -b "PlaySnd.c" -d SystemSevenOrLater
// Rez -a -o "Play Sound" -t osax -c ascr 'PlaySnd.r'
// Link -p -w -t osax -c ascr -rt osax=1000 -m PLAYSNDENTRY -sg ∂
//     "AEVTaevtplsn" -ra "AEVTaevtplsn"=resSysHeap,resLocked ∂
//     "PlaySnd.c.o" ∂
//     "{CLibraries}"StdCLib.o ∂
//     "{Libraries}"Runtime.o ∂
//     "{Libraries}"Interface.o ∂
//     -o "Play Sound"
//
///////////////////////////////////////////////////////////////

#include <Resources.h>
#include <Sound.h>
#include <AppleEvents.h>

#define kAsync          true        // asynchronous play
#define kQuietNow       true        // quiet channel now

#define kSndType        'snd '      // resource type we're
                                    //looking for
#define typeIntlText    'itxt'      // defined in AERegistry.r
#define typeStyledText  'STXT'      // defined in AERegistry.r
```

```
//////////////////////////////////////////////////////////////////
//
// PlaySndEntry ()
//
// The direct parameter is either a name or an ID of the 'snd '
// resource to play.
//
//////////////////////////////////////////////////////////////////

pascal OSErr PlaySndEntry( AppleEvent *theAEEvent,
                           AppleEvent *theReply,
                           long theRefCon)


{
    /* Function Prototypes */
     OSErr PlaySound(Handle theSoundHdl);

    /* variables */
    OSErr           theErr = noErr;
    DescType        typeCode;
    Size            sizeOfParam,
                    actualSize;
    Handle          theSndHandle = nil;  /*just clear our */
                                         /* sound handle*/
    SndChannelPtr   theSndChan = NULL;   /*NULL pointer to */
                                         /* a sound channel*/
    short           ourRezID = 0;
    Str255          ourRezName;
    FSSpec          ourSoundFile;
    short           ourFileRef, curResFile;

    /*
        Get the data type from direct object by using AESizeOfParam.
        We use this call instead of AEGetParamDesc or AEGetParamPtr
        because we are looking for one of several types. In this
```

```
way we can determine the type and move its data directly
into a variable instead of an AEDesc. Now we don't have to
worry about disposing of the AEDesc later.
*/


theErr = AESizeOfParam( theAEEvent,
                        keyDirectObject,
                        &typeCode,
                        &sizeOfParam);
if(theErr != noErr){
    /*
        If we fail here, just return the error. We don't need to
        do any cleanup, because we've allocated nothing on the
        heap yet. The Apple Event Manager automatically adds the
        error number to the reply as keyErrorNumber for nonzero
        handler returns.
    */

    return theErr;
}
else{
    if((typeCode == typeChar) || (typeCode == typeStyledText) ||
       (typeCode == typeIntlText)) {
        /*
            If one of these types match, we've been passed a name
            of a resource. Use AEGetParamPtr to move it into our
            string and transform it into a Pascal type string
            that we can pass to GetNamedResource. If we get an
            error in AEGetParamPtr, just let it fall through to
            the bottom of this handler.
        */
```

```
theErr = AEGetParamPtr(theAEEvent, keyDirectObject,
              typeChar, &typeCode, (Ptr)&ourRezName,
              sizeof(ourRezName), &actualSize);

if(theErr == noErr) {
   /* 'C' string has a null as last char */
   ourRezName[actualSize] = '\0';
   /* convert to Pascal string */
   c2pstr((char*) ourRezName);
   /* now grab the 'snd ' resource by name*/
   theSndHandle = GetNamedResource(kSndType,
                      (ConstStr255Param)ourRezName);
   /* check the error */
   theErr = ResError();
   if(theErr == noErr)
      theErr = PlaySound(theSndHandle);   /*call our */
                                          /* sound code*/
}
}
else {
   if(typeCode == typeLongInteger) {

      /*
         If we get a typeLongInteger, the user wants us to
         play a sound by its resource ID.

         AppleScript will send us a long here and the
         Resource Manager wants us to pass in a short, so
         let's have the Apple Event Manager coerce it to a
         short for us.
      */

      theErr = AEGetParamPtr(theAEEvent, keyDirectObject,
                 typeShortInteger, &typeCode,
                 (Ptr)&ourRezID, sizeof(ourRezID),
                 &actualSize);
```

```
    if(theErr == noErr) {
        /* now grab the 'snd ' resource by ID */
        theSndHandle = GetResource (kSndType, ourRezID);
        /* check the error */
        theErr = ResError();
        if(theErr == noErr)
            theErr = PlaySound(theSndHandle); /*call our */
                                              /* sound code*/

    }
}
else  {
    if(typeCode == typeAlias) {

        /*
            If we receive a typeAlias, the user is asking us
            to play a sound file. We want to use a FSSpec to
            open the resource file, so once again we ask the
            Apple Event Manager to coerce data to the type
            we need.
        */

        theErr = AEGetParamPtr(theAEEvent, keyDirectObject,
                    typeFSS, &typeCode,
                    (Ptr)&ourSoundFile,
                    sizeof(ourSoundFile),
                    &actualSize);
    if(theErr != noErr)
        return theErr;
        /* save off our current resource file */
    curResFile = CurResFile();

        /* open our resource file  for reading */
    ourFileRef = FSpOpenResFile(&ourSoundFile,
        fsRdPerm);
```

```
            /* check the error */
            theErr = ResError();
            if(theErr != noErr)
                return theErr;

            /* make our files resource fork top in the chain */
            UseResFile(ourFileRef);

            /*
                Since we don't know for sure the resource id of
                the targeted files 'snd ' resource, let's just
                get the first (and supposedly only) one.
            */

            theSndHandle = Get1IndResource(kSndType, 1);

            /* check the error */
            theErr = ResError();
            if(theErr == noErr)
                theErr = PlaySound(theSndHandle);

            /* restore resource chain and close our file */
            UseResFile(curResFile);
            CloseResFile(ourFileRef);
        }
        else /* wasn't a string, alias, or number so exit */
            return errAEEventNotHandled;
        }
    }
}
/* dispose 'snd ' handle if necessary */
if(theSndHandle != nil) ReleaseResource(theSndHandle);

return theErr;
}
```

```
////////////////////////////////////////////////////////////////
//
// PlaySound(Handle theSoundHdl)
//
// This is the code to play a 'snd '.
//
////////////////////////////////////////////////////////////////

OSErr PlaySound(Handle theSoundHdl)
  {
    /* our variables */
    OSErr      theErr = noErr;
    SndChannelPtr theSndChan = NULL; /*NULL pointer to a */
                                     /* sound channel*/

    /* open a channel so we can do synchronous play */
    theErr = SndNewChannel (&theSndChan, sampledSynth,
                  initMono, NULL);

    if (theErr == noErr) /* play that sound */
       theErr = SndPlay (theSndChan, theSoundHdl, !kAsync);

    /* dispose of the channel, if the sound channel was allocated */
    if (theSndChan != NULL)
       SndDisposeChannel(theSndChan, !kQuietNow);

    return theErr;
  }
```

```
/***********************************************


    Resource file for PlaySnd.c
    Copyright ®1993 Apple Computer Inc.
    All rights reserved.
    Written by Donald Olson


***********************************************/

#include "Types.r"
#include "SysTypes.r"
#include "AEUserTermTypes.r"

/* our version 1 and 2 resources */
resource 'vers' (1) {
    0x1,
    0x0,
    final,
    0x0,
    verUS,
    "1.0",
    "1.0, Copyright ® 1993 Apple Comput"
    "er, Inc. All rights reserved."
};

resource 'vers' (2) {
    0x1,
    0x0,
    final,
    0x0,
    verUS,
    "1.0",
    "(by Donald Olson)"
};
```

```
/*

    This string is used when the user double-clicks on a scripting
    addition file. Since it contains nothing that can be opened or
    printed, the user gets this in a dialog box (thanks to the
    system for making this happen).
*/


resource 'STR ' (-16397) {
    "This document can not be opened or printed."
    " It extends the functionality of AppleScript™"
    "and should be placed in the Scripting Additions"
    "folder found in the Extensions folder of your"
    " System Folder."
};


/*

    Our 'aete' resource. It's here that we describe to
    AppleScript the syntax of our scripting addition. Notice that
    the comment field contains information about the event and
    its parameters. These comments can be displayed by the
    Script Editor if the user selects this scripting addition in
    the terminology browser invoked when the user chooses the
    Open Dictionary menu.
*/


resource 'aete' (0, "Play Sound scripting addition") {
    0x0,
    -0x70,
    english,
    roman,
    {   /* array Suites: 1 elements */
        /* [1] */
        "System Object Suite",
        "",
        'syso',
```

```
1,
1,
{   /* array Events: 1 elements */
    /* [1] */
    "play sound",
    " This is the syntax for invoking this scripting"
    " addition from AppleScript™.",
    'aevt',
    'plsn',
    noReply,
    "The reply is not required",
    replyOptional,
    singleItem,
    notEnumerated,
    reserved,
    reserved,
    reserved,
    reserved,
    reserved,
    reserved,
    reserved,
    reserved,
    reserved,
    reserved,
    reserved,
    reserved,
    reserved,
    '****',
    "id or name of 'snd ' resource to play"
    " or  path to a sound file",
    directParamRequired,
    singleItem,
    notEnumerated,
    doesntChangeState,
    reserved,
```

```
        reserved,
        reserved,
        reserved,
        reserved,
        reserved,
        reserved,
        reserved,
        reserved,
        reserved,
        reserved,
        reserved,
        {   /* array OtherParams: 0 elements */
        }
    },
    {  /* array Classes: 0 elements */
    },
    {  /* array ComparisonOps: 0 elements */
    },
    {  /* array Enumerations: 0 elements */
    }
    }
};
```

# Scripting Additions at a Glance

This appendix summarizes the commands described in this guide and the placeholders used in syntax descriptions. For more detailed information about these commands, see Chapter 2, "Scripting Addition Commands."

## Scripting Addition Commands

Table A-1 beginning on page 106 summarizes the scripting addition commands described in this guide and their syntax.

**Table A-1**    Command syntax for standard AppleScript scripting additions

continued

| Command | Syntax | Result |
|---|---|---|
| activate | activate *referenceToApplication* | None |
| ASCII character | ASCII character *integer* | String |
| ASCII number | ASCII number *string* | Integer |
| beep | beep | None |
| | beep *integer* | None |
| choose application | choose application | Reference |
| | choose application ⌐<br>with prompt *dialogString* | |
| | choose application ⌐<br>application label *dialogString* | |
| | choose application ⌐⌐<br>with prompt *dialogString*<br>application label *dialogString* | |
| choose file | choose file | Reference |
| | choose file with prompt *dialogString* | |
| | choose file of type *listOfTypes* | |
| | choose file with prompt *dialogString* ⌐<br>of type *listOfTypes* | |
| choose folder | choose folder | Reference |
| | choose folder with prompt *dialogString* | |
| close access | close access *referenceToFile* | Error code |
| current date | current date | Date |

**Table A-1**   Command syntax for standard AppleScript scripting additions (continued)

| Command | Syntax | Result |
|---|---|---|
| display dialog | display dialog *dialogString*<br>[ default answer *dialogString* ]<br>[ buttons *buttonList* ]<br>[ default button *integer* \| *dialogString* ]<br>[ with icon *integer* \| *dialogString* ] | Record with two properties, Button Returned (a string) and Text Returned (a string) |
| get eof | get eof *referenceToFile* | Integer |
| info for | info for *referenceToFile* | File Info record |
| list disks | list disks | List of strings |
| list folder | list folder *referenceToFolder* | List of strings |
| load script | load script *referenceToFile* | Script object |
| log | log *string* | None |
| new file | new file | Reference |
| | new file with prompt *dialogString* | |
| | new file default name *dialogString* | |
| | new file with prompt *dialogString*<br>default name *dialogString* | |
| offset | offset of *string* in *string* | Integer |
| open for access | open for access *referenceToFile* | File reference number |
| | open for access *referenceToFile*<br>write permission *Boolean* | |
| path to | path to *folderOrApplication* | Alias or string |
| | path to *folderOrApplication*<br>as *className* | |

*continued*

**Table A-1**   Command syntax for standard AppleScript scripting additions (continued)

| Command | Syntax | | Result |
|---|---|---|---|
| random number | random number <br> [ *number* ] <br> [ from *number* to *number* ] <br> [ with seed *number* ] | ⌐ <br> ⌐ <br> ⌐ | Integer or real value |
| read | read *referenceToFile* <br> [ from *integer* ] <br> [ for *integer* \| to *integer* <br> \| until *string* \| before *string* ] <br> [ as *className* <br> [ using delimiter[s] *delimiters* ]] | ⌐ <br> ⌐ <br> ⌐ <br> ⌐ <br> ⌐ | Requested data |
| round | round *number* | | Integer |
| round | round *number* <br> rounding ( up \| down \| <br> toward zero \| to nearest ) | ⌐ <br> ⌐ | |
| run script | run script *referenceOrString* | ⌐ | Value returned by script <br> that is run |
| | run script *referenceOrString* <br> with parameters *listOfParameters* | ⌐ | |
| | run script *referenceOrString* <br> in *scriptingComponent* | ⌐ | |
| | run script *referenceOrString* <br> with parameters *listOfParameters* <br> in *scriptingComponent* | ⌐ <br> ⌐ | |
| scripting components | scripting components | | List of strings |
| set eof | set eof *referenceToFile* to *integer* | | None |
| start log | start log | | None |
| stop log | stop log | | None |

*continued*

**Table A-1**    Command syntax for standard AppleScript scripting additions (continued)

| Command | Syntax | Result |
|---|---|---|
| store script | store script *scriptObjectVariable* | None |
| | store script *scriptObjectVariable* in *referenceToFile* | |
| | store script *scriptObjectVariable* replacing ( ask \| yes \| no ) | |
| | store script *scriptObjectVariable* in *referenceToFile* replacing ( ask \| yes \| no ) | |
| time to GMT | time to GMT | Integer |
| write | write *dataToWrite* to *referenceToFile* | None |
| | write *dataToWrite* to *referenceToFile* for *integer* | |
| | write *dataToWrite* to *referenceToFile* starting at *integer* | |
| | write *dataToWrite* to *referenceToFile* for *integer* starting at *integer* | |

# Placeholders

Table A-2 explains the placeholders used in the syntax descriptions in this appendix.

**Table A-2**    Placeholders used in syntax descriptions

| Placeholder | Explanation |
|---|---|
| *Boolean* | An expression that evaluates to `true` or `false`. |
| *buttonList* | A list of strings, each of which represents a button in a dialog box. The maximum number of characters in each string is 255. You can specify up to three buttons. |
| *className* | A class identifier or an expression that evaluates to an object class identifier. |
| *dataToWrite* | Data of an appropriate type to be written to a specified file. |
| *delimiters* | String or constant specifying a delimiter, or a two-item list of strings or constants. |
| *dialogString* | A string of up to 255 characters. |
| *folderOrApplication* | One of these constants: `apple menu`, `apple menu items`, `control panels`, `desktop`, `extensions`, `preferences`, `printmonitor`, `printmonitor documents`, `trash`, `startup items`, `system folder`, `temporary items`, `startup disk`, `frontmost application`. |
| *integer* | An expression that evaluates to an integer. |
| *listOfParameters* | A list of parameters to be passed to the target's Run handler. |
| *listOfTypes* | A list of strings, each of which is a four-character file type code that identifies a particular type, such as `"TEXT"`, `"APPL"`, `"PICT"`, or `"PNTG"`. |

*continued*

**Table A-2**    Placeholders used in syntax descriptions (continued)

| Placeholder | Explanation |
|---|---|
| *nameString* | A string of the form<br>"*Disk:Folder1:Folder2:...:Filename*". |
| *number* | An expression that evaluates to an integer or real number. |
| *referenceOrString* | A reference of the form `file` *nameString* or `alias` *nameString*, or a string that consists of a valid script. |
| *referenceToApplication* | A reference of the form `application` "*Disk:Folder1:Folder2:...:ApplicationName*". |
| *referenceToFile* | A reference of the form `file` *nameString* or `alias` *nameString*. |
| *referenceToFolder* | A reference of the form `file` *nameString*, `alias` *nameString*, or `folder` *nameString* that specifies a folder or an alias to a folder. |
| *scriptObjectVariable* | A variable whose value is a script object. |
| *scriptingComponent* | A string that consists of the name of a scripting component. |
| *string* | An expression that evaluates to a string. |

# Index

## T

## U

## V

## W, X, Y, Z

This Apple manual was written, edited, and composed on a desktop publishing system using Apple Macintosh computers and FrameMaker software. Proof pages were created on an Apple LaserWriter II$_{\text{NTX}}$ printer. Final page negatives were output directly from the text and graphic files. Line art was created using Adobe™ Illustrator. PostScript™, the page-description language for the LaserWriter, was developed by Adobe Systems Incorporated.

Text type is Palatino® and display type is Helvetica®. Bullets are ITC Zapf Dingbats®. Some elements, such as program listings, are set in Apple Courier.

WRITERS
Sean Cotter and Pegi Wheeler

DEVELOPMENTAL EDITOR
Jeanne Woodward

ILLUSTRATOR
Deborah Dennis

PRODUCTION EDITOR
Rex Wolf

Special thanks to Donald Olson.

Acknowledgments to Scott Bongiorno, Ron Karr, Yuji Hachiya, Jon Pugh, Brett Sher, and the entire AppleScript team.